A child who is loved
will in turn be able to love.

Warm thanks to my fellow quilters:
A. Alessandri, D. Amsden, I. Boccucci, D. Calderini, G. Campanini,
R. Faroldi, V. Grassi, M. Jordan, F. Morini, G. Musiari, S. Ognibene,
R. Ranieri, E. Santini, M.L Sassi, J. Theobald, P. Visioli, I. Wieland

Thanks also to
Manifatture Govi, Magazzini Coin, Parma Patchwork Club, G. Napodano,
and to my friends M.L Monici and I. Berni for the amusing cakes.

Photographs by Alberto Bertoldi and Mario Matteucci

Graphic design and layout by
Paola Masera and Amelia Verga
with Beatrice Brancaccio

Translation by Chiara Tarsia

Library of Congress Cataloging-in-Publication Data Available

10 9 8 7 6 5 4 3 2 1

Published by Sterling Publishing Company, Inc.
387 Park Avenue South, New York, N.Y. 10016
Originally published in Italy under the title *Baby Patchwork* and
© 1996 by R.C.S. Libri S.p.A.
English translation © 1999 by Sterling Publishing Company, Inc.
Distributed in Canada by Sterling Publishing
C/o Canadian Manda Group, One Atlantic Avenue, Suite 105
Toronto, Ontario, Canada M6K 3E7
Distributed in Great Britain and Europe by Cassell PLC
Wellington House, 125 Strand, London WC2R 0BB, England
Distributed in Australia by Capricorn Link (Australia) Pty Ltd.
P.O. Box 6651, Baulkham Hills, Business Centre, NSW 2153, Australia
Printed in Hong Kong
All rights reserved

Sterling ISBN 0-8069-9951-9

BABY
PATCHWORK

TABLE OF CONTENTS

BIG IDEAS FOR SMALL PRESENTS

PROJECT PATTERNS

PREFACE

On the full-size quilt opposite, a cross-stitched alphabet-block center is framed by a variety of pieced borders. (G. Musiani)

You are probably anxious to get started and might be inclined to jump right into making a project, but please read all of the introductory material first and let the beautiful photographs serve to inspire you.

Baby Patchwork provides designs and ideas for creating delightful hand-made gifts for all those special little someones in your life. It features a piecing technique that you may not be familiar with, but one that you may find surprisingly easier than most. This new technique uses tracing paper!

I have intentionally placed the tracing-paper method last in this book, so that you can compare it with the more traditional techniques that precede it. Whether you're a beginner or an experienced quilter, the tracing-paper method may be for you.

One last piece of advice: Please read the Basics and Patchwork Techniques sections, as well as the introduction to the Projects section, before starting to make any of the quilts – and be sure to read the directions for any project all the way through before beginning the work.

For Baby's bedroom: a small panel appliquéd with Baby's first initial and date of birth. (A. Alessandri)

6

MORE THAN PATCHWORK

This lively tablecloth is made up of pieced squares with appliquéd tulips. (A. Alessandri) On the left are two boxes covered in a Log Cabin motif.

My previous books[1] have dealt broadly with the subject of patchwork, so it gives me particular pleasure to present in *Baby Patchwork* a collection of quilts that were inspired by, created for, and dedicated to children, who, like quilts, thrive with love, devotion, and patience.

I find it fascinating to recognize in quilts both old and new the literal and figurative depictions of nature, historical events, holidays, personal milestones, and hobbies, or whatever else the quiltmakers' creativity in every country has produced.

I find it comforting to see worldwide appreciation of the beauty of nature, love of country, and family affection that has inspired many designs.

For me, however, the greatest pleasure lies in discovering the inspiration behind the design and in identifying the hand of a loving quilter among the strong or subtle colors of a mini-quilt; its ingenious motifs of flowers, animals, and toys; and all the other myriad elements of the design.

That was my first reason for creating *Baby Patchwork*. The second was my observation that many quilters, particularly beginners, prefer working on small projects rather than larger ones, such as a full-size bed quilt.

This book, which is intended for both novice and experienced quilters alike, provides ideas for making very special personal additions to that very special child's life. Imagine saying "I love you" with a soft, cuddly, handmade quilt. The book also offers suggestions for decorating children's clothes, bibs, and bags with loving originality. You will find some fun things included, too, such as ornaments and toys.

My hope is that you will allow the projects, photographs, and ideas in *Baby Patchwork* to inspire you to create your own quilted "I love you" for all of the special children in your life.

[1] *Patchwork - History, techniques, suggestions* ed. Fabbri
Patchwork Quilts ed. Fabbri

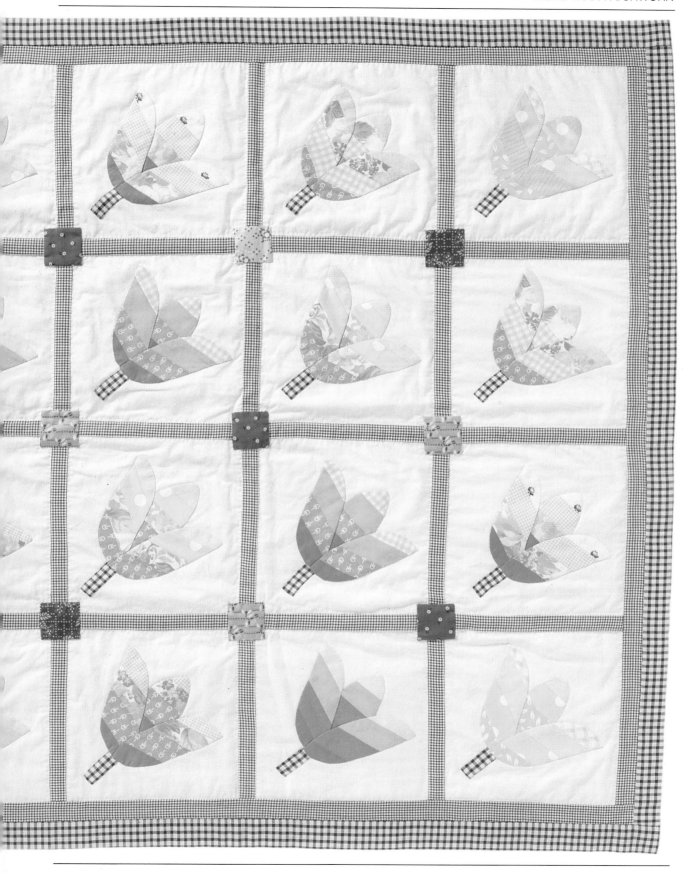

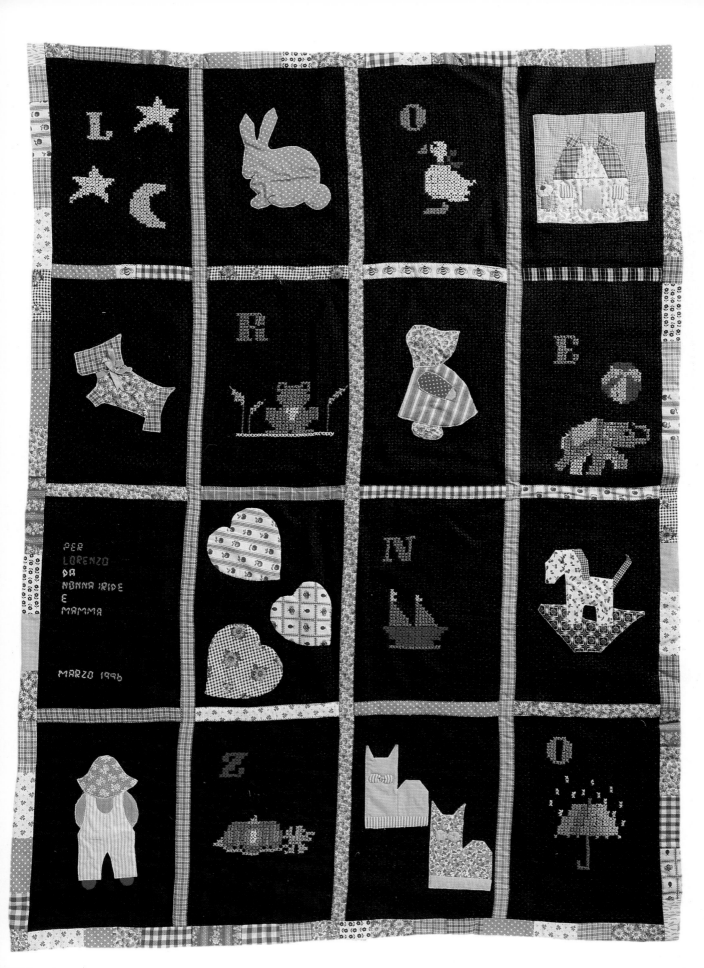

A quilt may be described in many ways: a piece of handiwork consisting of two layers of fabric sandwiched around one single or multiple layer of padding; a way of using up odd pieces of fabric; a means of creative expression; as an excuse to pass the time in the pleasant, congenial company of other quilters; and so on.

A mini-quilt for Baby is above all, however, a token of love as well as something to keep a little one warm. It is not only a companion for Baby, who will be stimulated by its colors, intrigued by its designs, and will fall asleep wrapped in its cozy softness, but also an accessory whose decorative top will appeal to an adult's taste as part of the decor of Baby's room.

If Baby should want to pluck the flowers or grasp the hearts, teddy bears, or bunnies (all firmly attached, appliqué style) from the quilt top or to constantly keep it near when playing at home or out for an airing, don't worry. If the quilt should get ruined, just think of the pleasure you can have making a replacement.

Baby quilts are an American tradition dating back to the early part of the twentieth century. Until then quiltmakers never considered making scaled-down versions for children because the hardships of pioneer life made it necessary for all members of a household, adults and children alike, to sleep together in one large bed.

It was only when children were no longer perceived as miniature adults and more attention was paid to their special needs, including separate beds, that mini-quilts evolved along with the motifs so dear to a child's imagination − animals, flowers, toys, letters of the alphabet, storybook characters, and so on.

At the center of this multipurpose bag is a patchwork-framed stenciled duckling. (G. Berti)

At right, this sporty outfit has appliquéd patchwork hearts that give it a personal touch. (G. Berti)

Opposite, a mini-quilt made of knit blocks is adorned with appliquéd and cross-stitched motifs.

Sunbonnet Sue and Overall Sam, typical children of the American prairies, were characters first designed for children's reading books, but they quickly became favorites for appliquéd baby quilts.

In creating quilt tops and other pieces of handiwork, I too have often used these classic early American motifs, adapting them to suit my own taste, because I am partial to pastels, particularly the soft pinks and blues traditionally used for little girls' and boys' quilts.

In addition to offering you my own modest designs, I am pleased to also present the work of other quiltmakers, which enables *Baby Patchwork* to provide a wide range of ideas and inspirations. As a mother myself, and also a grandmother, I know that nothing is too beautiful, sweet, or rich in meaning for our precious little ones, so I've included designs in which traditional patchwork is combined with other, newer techniques.

Classic patchwork designs have been enhanced by rouched lace, stenciling, and cross-stitching. Crazy quilts have been decorated with multicolored embroidery. A Log Cabin motif has become a frame for a photo of Baby reproduced on fabric. Even felt animal appliqués that have been traced from patterned fabric are used to embellish a quilt.

I hope that the ideas in this book will act as a springboard for your own ingenuity, resulting in beautiful, personalized, love-filled quilt creations.

Patience and precision are essential in quiltmaking, but please don't feel discouraged if your project turns out to be less than absolutely perfect. If you (or some eagle-eyed observer) should spot a mistake that you made in design or workmanship, you can console yourself by aligning with the early American quiltmakers who intentionally worked a mistake into each quilt as an attempt to avoid incurring Divine wrath. They believed that their God would surely punish the presumptiveness of any mere mortal who strove for the perfection that traditionally belonged to Him alone.

If you want to make something really sweet for that special little person in your life, why not use your ingenuity to "bake" Baby an unmistakably sweet gift that you can stitch in patchwork (or appliqué) and that Baby will be able to enjoy again and again? It could be a simple pie with an appliquéd apple or teddy bear, or hearts embroidered on a soft "marzipan" base, or a brilliant star shining against a background of satiny white cake "icing," or a crazy-quilt cake whose multicolored patches are hand-stitched with almond "paste."

To all of you readers and quilters, I send my very best wishes for enjoyable and successful projects – or, to use the quilters' customary phrase, HAPPY QUILTING!!

A reproduced photo image on white fabric makes up the center patch in the Log Cabin motif on this photo album. (G. Berti)

This cake to celebrate Baby's first birthday is covered with cream-colored "icing." It features an "almond-paste" star at the center and is encircled by a plump, snow-white "icing" braid.

The most popular motif in mini-quilting decorates this little "quilted" cake made to commemorate a very special birthday; the birthday child can give the hearts (which are attached with hook-and-loop dots) as party favors to family and friends who come to celebrate.

At right, this hanging holder features patchwork pockets embellished with appliqué and cross-stitch. (A. Alessandri)

THE HISTORY OF PATCHWORK

TERMINOLOGY

In many books and magazines, the terms patchwork and quilting are used interchangeably. In some countries (mostly the United States), the entire quiltmaking process and all of its various techniques are collectively referred to as quilting. In other countries (mostly in Europe), it is all called patchwork. This can be confusing to a beginner, so it may be helpful to look at the terms as they are used in this book. What I call patchwork is the process in which fabric shapes are cut out and then joined together with stitches. It can be done in a number of different techniques. Quilting is the technique of decoratively stitching together a top fabric, padding (today most quilts use synthetic batting), and a backing.

ORIGINS

Some historians believe that Western civilization had its origin along the Nile River, others claim it was born along the river Ganges, and still others are convinced that it was in the Valley of the Tigris and Euphrates Rivers that it began. Regardless, over the years evidence has emerged in each of these places that the local people knew simple patchwork techniques and that these techniques were widespread in the Near East in countries such as Persia, Egypt, and ancient Rome.

The quiltmaking techniques used today took centuries to evolve, going through many permutations over the ages. The Crusades had a major effect by introducing the idea of layering fabrics for warmth. The Cavaliers who returned home from the Near East had learned that wearing padded, multilayered garments underneath their armor protected them from the harsh cold of winter − as well as from their own chain mail.

Back home their European wives soon learned the advantages of layering and padding, then adapted the techniques for doing it and made them their own. As time went on, the placement of the stitches that held together the padded layers became more regular and the patches themselves became less random in terms of color and layout. As a result, quilts became not just useful but decorative, too. Quiltmaking was widespread on five continents, but the most significant schools of the art were in the United States and England.

PATCHWORK IN EUROPE

By introducing its own enriching touches to patchwork, every country has throughout the centuries contributed to the development of quiltmaking and enabled it to evolve from a totally utilitarian process to an artistic means of expression.

The French, for example, introduced the technique, called appliqué, of cutting figures from one fabric and sewing them onto a different one.

Seamstresses from the northern European countries specialized in the making of knit coverlets.

In Italy, too, patchwork became popular, although it never quite became as enduring a tradition it was in other countries. Famous Italian patchworks include the Florentine quilt, the rich costumes made throughout the centuries for the Palio in Siena and the gorgeous silk coverlets created in Sicily.

This soft blue-and-white panel with appliquéd hearts was made for use as a headboard. (G. Berti)

PATCHWORK IN ENGLAND

Among the European countries patchwork reached a pinnacle in England that was unsurpassed until the seamstresses of the New World added their ingenuity.

It is probably not difficult to imagine just how much the warmth of padded covers was appreciated in an age and climate where the cold reigned.

At first poor peasants used all kinds of fabric scraps, both old and new, for their patchwork, but with the passing of time, as well as the rise in wealth and increase in experience of the quiltmakers, quilt tops became increasingly more varied in pattern and refined in execution. Quilts eventually made their way into the houses and castles of the aristocracy, where wealthy women greatly valued them as works of art and often indulged in designing and making their own, often adding new elements of refinement. Other factors that contributed to the evolution of patchwork were the importing of raw materials for making fabrics and the introduction of machines for spinning, weaving, and sewing. The numerous beautiful works from nineteenth-century England earned for Queen Victoria's reign the nickname "Golden Age of Patchwork."

The most treasured pieces were often willed to descendants. They were coveted as highly as priceless gems and, as such, were handed down from generation to generation.

Quilting was also taught in schools and it frequently became a family business in which everyone took part. The children usually performed the easiest tasks, such as threading the needles, while the men would get the looms ready, cut out wood or metal templates for the patches, and draft the preliminary designs.

Eventually, economic hard times gave rise to a new profession: the wandering quilter, who would live and work in someone else's home for as long as her skill was required (and she was paid according to the amount of thread used!) and then move on with her loom and experience in tow. Then another occupation arose in support of the quilters: the markers. When the design of a quilt was particularly complex and demanding, a specialist would be called in to trace it onto the fabric.

After a while English quilting began to lose its creative momentum, but it never died out completely. In fact, it found new life in the colonies of the United States, where it was introduced by European immigrants. Since then it has bounced back and forth between the New and Old Worlds in a continuous artistic exchange that continues even today.

This delightful little coverlet combines warm and cool colors in a harmonious whole, using geometric and whimsical motifs. (J. Theobald from the Quiltmaker magazine)

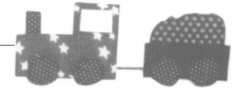

PATCHWORK IN AMERICA

European – particularly French, English, and Dutch – migration to the United States gave rise to a new social reality in which women made their own coverlets and garments. Under such circumstances quiltmaking, which was already widespread in Europe, became an American occupation. The colonists had to make do with whatever resources were readily available, and they frugally recycled whatever remained of old covers brought over from Europe as well as well-worn clothes and flour, seed, or feeding sacks. The materials they used for padding their quilts was initially crude and included dry leaves from trees or corn and even pieces of paper.

Years passed before the colonies were able to raise cotton or sheep to provide the most common natural padding fibers used today, but having the fibers and turning them into usable batting were two different things. The first American wool batting, when it was wet, used to smell like – well, sheep. Similarly, the first cotton batting, which usually still had seeds inside it, wasn't nearly as smooth as its modern counterparts.

For many years housewives dyed their own fibers and did spinning and weaving with whatever they could find in their immediate surroundings, such as herbs, flowers, or minerals.

QUILTING BEES

Patchwork was done just about everywhere in the United States, and it acquired a social aspect with the advent of the quilting bee (or quilting party), an already established tradition in England that came to have even more significance in the New World.

For a family of colonists or pioneers, a quilting bee was a very important event. It was one of those rare occasions when chores were abandoned in favor of spending a pleasant day among congenial company. To make the occasion even more special, women would put on their Sunday-best clothes before gathering at the home of a friend or relative to work communally on a quilt that was being created as a gift for an upcoming wedding, as a present of welcome for a newcomer, or as a good-bye token for someone about to move away. The quilting bee was an opportunity to really feel like part of the community; it provided a sense of solidarity and common purpose, something particularly important to people whose very survival often depended on mutual cooperation.

At right, appliquéd and pieced blocks are joined in a bright/dark checkerboard pattern. The blocks are decorated with traditional and whimsical motifs. (I. Wieland)

Below, a banner made of squares featuring traditional geometric motifs. (Coin)

COMPARING AMERICAN AND ENGLISH PATCHWORK

There is no doubt that the work produced in the New World differed greatly from that produced in England. Technically speaking, the quilts of the new Americans were more modest, but they were also rich in creativity and symbolism. The differences in lifestyle on the two continents also determined an important difference in the assembly of the quilt top. In England the patchwork top was often made starting with a central motif first, then adding patches until the desired pattern and size were achieved. In the United States a new method evolved: that of making many individual blocks and then joining them together to make a quilt top.

It was practicality that led to the American construction method. Most people in the new United States lived in very small quarters, and a large project would have been much more cumbersome to work on in a small one-room cabin than in a large English sitting room. In addition, small-scale projects were convenient to work and easy to quickly lay aside for working in the field or making long journeys by covered wagon.

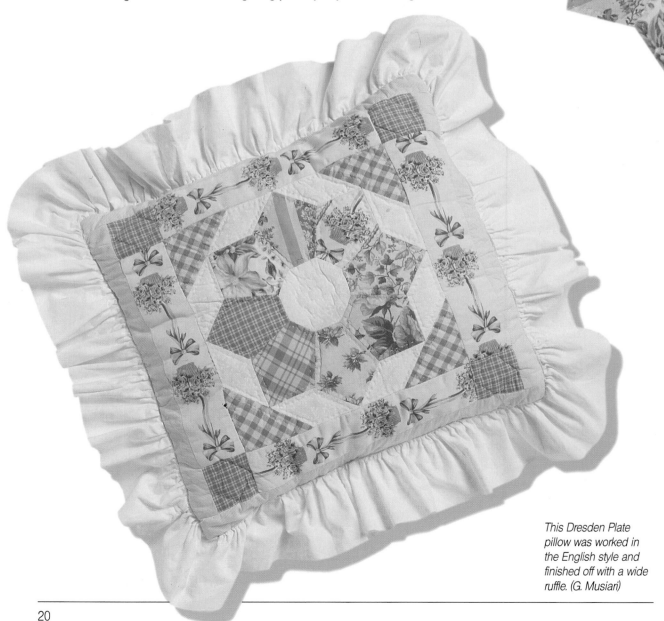

This Dresden Plate pillow was worked in the English style and finished off with a wide ruffle. (G. Musiari)

Many distinctive patchwork patterns were created and named, the inspiration for which came from a wide variety of sources: religion, home, family, friends, special occasions and interests, nature, and more.

Among the most popular and enduring motifs are the versatile Log Cabin, Pinwheel, Basket, Birds in Flight, Ocean Waves, and a wide range of Star variations that include the Ohio Star, Morning Star, and Star of Friendship, to name just a few. Animals, trees, flowers, and hearts have always been favorites.

The methods of one group of quiltmakers intermingled with those of other groups generate a constant newness in the development of designs and techniques that are handed down from generation to generation.

The nineteenth century was without doubt the most significant period in American quiltmaking, but the development of this art that has endured through the ages has also reflected the history of the United States from colonial to modern times. We have a rich legacy of know-how and beauty that keeps motivating quilters the world over to continually achieve new heights.

This pretty patchwork pillow was worked in the American style. (G. Berti)

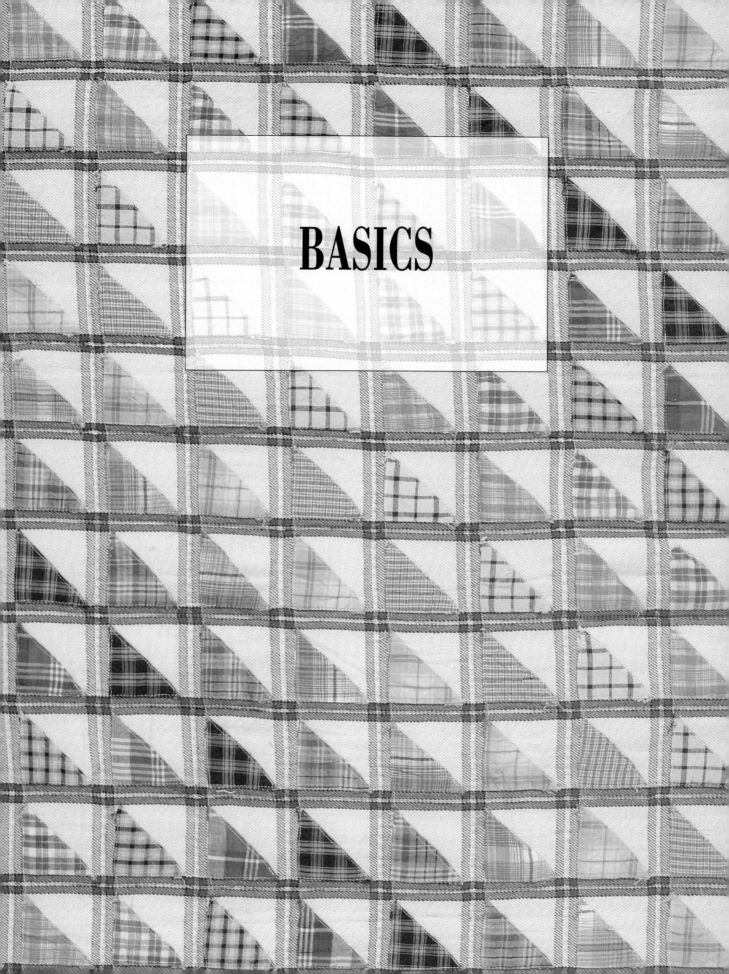

BASICS

TOOLS AND EQUIPMENT

Basic quiltmaking equipment includes a sewing machine and iron plus the following:
- needles for hand- and machine-stitching, appliqué, and embroidery;
- pins, as fine and pointed as possible – long flat-headed pins made specifically for quilting are the best;
- marking pencils for making templates and marking patterns; colored pencils or crayons for planning the colors; tailor's chalk and disappearing-ink pens for marking the quilt top;
- embroidery or quilting hoop or frame – adjustable ones are the most versatile;
- rotary cutter and self-healing cutting mat;
- transparent plastic quilting rulers, triangles, and squares;
- tracing paper or acetate.
Novice quiltmakers can begin by using the general sewing equipment they already have on hand and then acquire more specialized tools little by little as their experience and expertise increase.

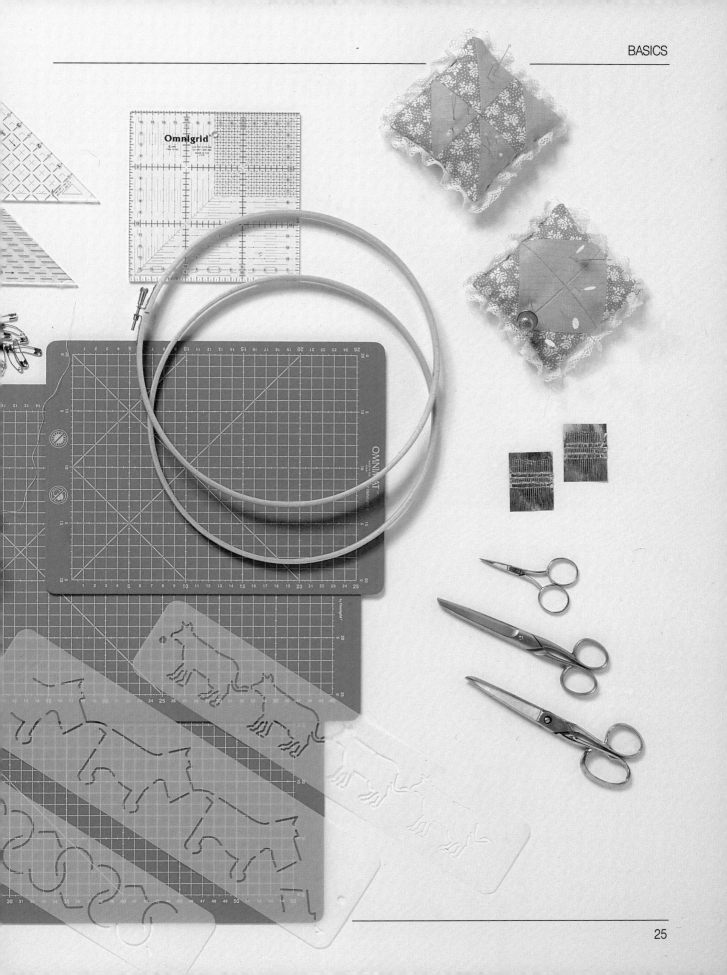

FABRIC

At right, this little water-color quilt was made with delicate nuances of shading. The quilting adds a fine decorative touch to the simple square patches. (D. Amsden)

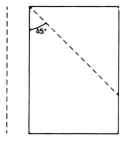

Straight and bias grains

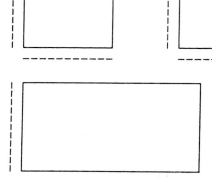

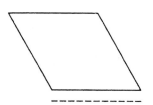

Straight-grain geometric patches

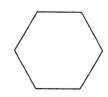

Any type of fabric can be used for patchwork, but for quilts intended for Baby, the best without a doubt is 100% cotton. Before cutting, soak each fabric separately in hot water to both preshrink and check for colorfastness. Iron the fabric before cutting and while it is still damp; do it with great care because ironing out set-in creases at a later stage will be impossible.

It is advisable to plan the cutting of the patches according to the grain of the fabric in order to avoid elasticity in your project where it doesn't belong. Cutting on the straight grain (either lengthwise or crosswise) provides the least stretching; cutting on the bias (45 degrees off the straight grain) provides the most. Always remove the selvages first.

CUTTING

MATERIALS

- rotary cutter
- self-healing cutting mat
- a long, clear-plastic quilting ruler with angle markings of 30°, 45°, and 65°
- a clear-plastic quilting square

Before cutting out patches, count the number needed from each fabric in order to determine the best cutting method for each fabric. For relatively few patches, cut them out one at a time. For a large number of patches, a method consisting of the following three steps is usually the quickest:
- squaring the fabric;
- cutting strips;
- cutting strips into patches.

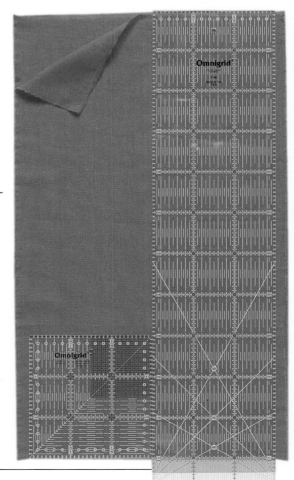

SQUARING THE FABRIC

- After the selvages have been cut away, it is important to square the remaining fabric because its edges, even if the fabric has been cut or torn along the grain, are never perfectly perpendicular.
- Fold the fabric in half (if it is wider or longer than the cutting mat and ruler).
- Prepare to do the cutting standing up.

- Place the fabric on the cutting mat with the side to be cut along the right-hand side.
- Position the ruler vertically on the fabric with one short plastic edge along the bottom edge of the fabric (for extra precision also line up the transparent quilting square with the bottom edge of the fabric; after the

ruler has been properly positioned, remove the square).
- Holding down the ruler firmly with your left hand, start cutting from bottom to top (away from you), moving your left hand along the ruler as the cutter approaches your fingers.
- Remove the excess fabric strip that has been cut away.

CUTTING STRIPS ON THE STRAIGHT GRAIN

- Place the squared fabric on the cutting mat so that the edge to be cut is at left.
- Determine the desired width of the strip, line up the ruler and hold it down firmly with your left hand, then cut.
- Set aside the strip and line up the ruler to cut the next one. To determine the cut width of a strip, add a seam allowance of ¹/₂" (1.25 cm) to the desired finished width. If many strips are needed, stop occasionally, check that the strips are still straight and their edges perpendicular, and then repeat the squaring process if necessary.

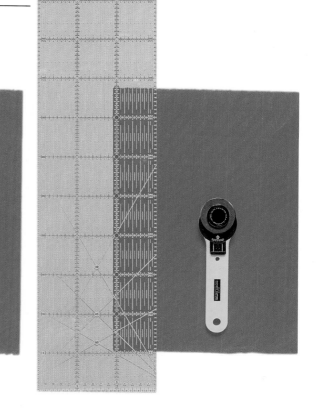

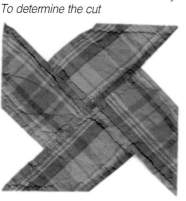

CUTTING STRIPS ON THE BIAS

- Line up the ruler against the bottom edge of the fabric along the 45° angle line. If you aren't sure you will have enough fabric to cut all the patches, you can cut them instead at an angle of 30° or 60°.

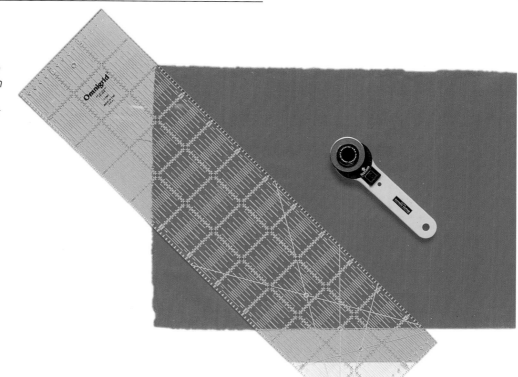

CUTTING STRIPS INTO PATCHES

Before discussing the various patch-cutting techniques used to make the projects in this book, I want to first point out that the basic geometric shapes usually used in patchwork are squares, rectangles, and parallelograms. From these are derived right-angle and equilateral triangles as well as hexagons.

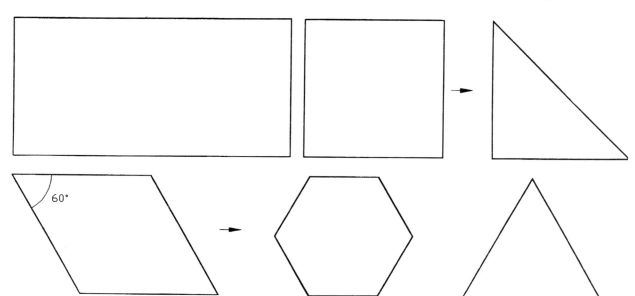

SQUARES

- Square the strip. Place the edge to be cut at left. Line up the ruler at the desired measurement, then cut.
- Occasionally check that the strip is straight, using the transparent square. To determine the cut size of a square patch, add ½" (1.25 cm) to both the length and width of the finished patch. If each edge of the finished patch should be 2 ½" (6 cm), the cut edges of the patch should each be 3" (7.5 cm).

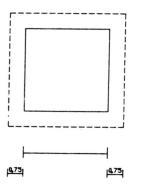

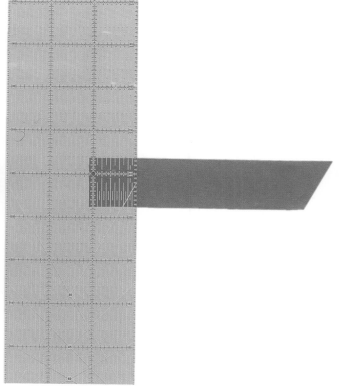

HALF-SQUARE TRIANGLES

To cut half-square right-angle triangles, cut a square along its diagonal. To determine the cut size of the square, add 1" (2.5 cm) to one short edge of the finished triangle. If the short edge of the finished patch should be 2" (5 cm), the cut edge of the patch should be 3" (7.5 cm).

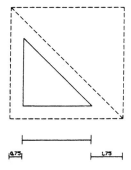

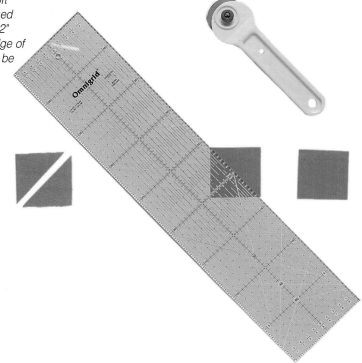

QUARTER-SQUARE TRIANGLES

To cut quarter-square right-angle triangles, cut a square along both of its diagonals. To determine the cut size of the square, add 1 ½" (3.75 cm) to the long edge of the finished triangle. If the long edge of the finished patch should be 2" (5 cm), the cut edge of the patch should be 3 ½" (8.75 cm).

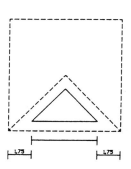

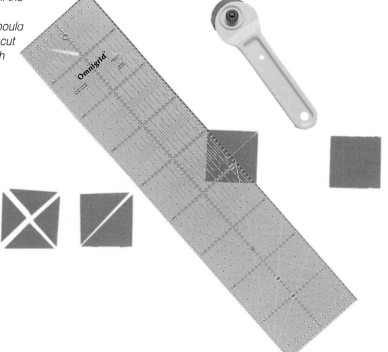

RECTANGLES

To cut a rectangle, follow the same basic procedure as for cutting a square, but line up the ruler at the bottom of the rectangle instead of the side of the square. To determine the cut size of the rectangle, add ½" (1.25 cm) to both the length and width of the finished patch. If the size of the finished patch should be 1" x 2" (2.5 x 5 cm), the cut size of the patch should each be 1 ½" x 2 ½" (3.75 x 6.25 cm).

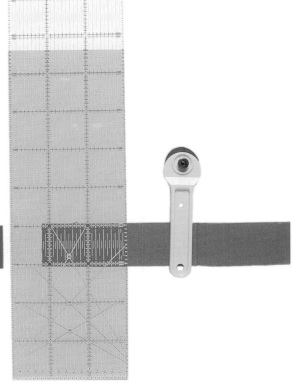

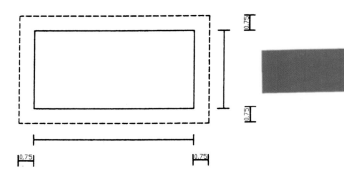

PARALLELOGRAMS

To cut a parallelogram from a strip, use the 30°, 45°, or 60° angled lines on the ruler.
- Lay the strip across the cutting mat with the shorter edges at the sides.
- Line up the ruler along the desired angle line, then cut.
- Line up the ruler parallel to the first cut, then cut again.
To determine the cut length, add 1" (2.5 cm) to the length of the finished patch. If the length of the finished patch should be 2" (5 cm), the cut length of the patch should be 3" (7.5 cm).

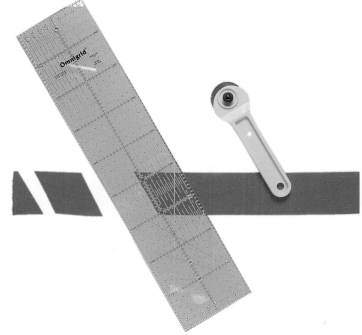

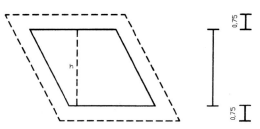

HEXAGONS

To cut a hexagon (or any other straight-edged geometric shape), the following simple but accurate method works very well:

- Cut out a paper template the same shape and size as the cut patch (the finished size plus seam allowance).
- Stick the template to the underside of a transparent ruler with clear fusible web tape.
- Line up the ruler and template on the fabric and cut one edge of the patch.
- Rotate the template to match up the next edge of the patch, then cut.
- Rotate the template as needed to cut the remaining edges of the patch.

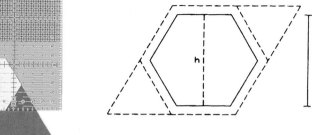

For those who want a quilting shortcut, there are patchwork kits available on the market. They come with fabric and patterns (some include precut templates or patches) and complete instructions for how to make the project. Usually kits have helpful photos or diagrams, especially one of the finished project.

SEWING

To use the Quick & Easy method, it is necessary to have a sewing machine with a presser foot the same width as the desired seam allowance or a seam guide. If your machine has neither, you can stick a piece of colored tape on the plate at the desired distance from where the needle enters the fabric. If many patches will be made, join them with assembly-line stitching, which will save both time and thread. To make a quilt with uniform blocks, it is advisable to make a sample block first and then cut the rest of the pieces in series and assembly-line-stitch them together.

Colored tape is used as a guide for uniformly sewing at the desired distance.

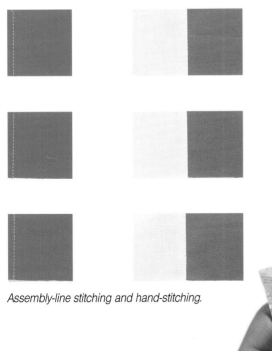

Assembly-line stitching and hand-stitching.

PRESSING

A Log Cabin motif adorns the lid of this gift box made entirely of fabric. (G. Berti)

- It is advisable to press each seam before it is crossed by the next one; you may be able to finger-press some seams instead of using an iron.
- Press seam allowance toward darker fabrics wherever they might show through lighter patches.
- Pressing all seam allowances toward the same direction makes the piece sturdier.

- Pressing the seams open makes the piece lie flatter, but the batting could poke through to the outside between stitches. I have come across many different hints for pressing seams that frequently contradict each other, so I learned that experience is the best teacher in deciding which method works best in any given situation.

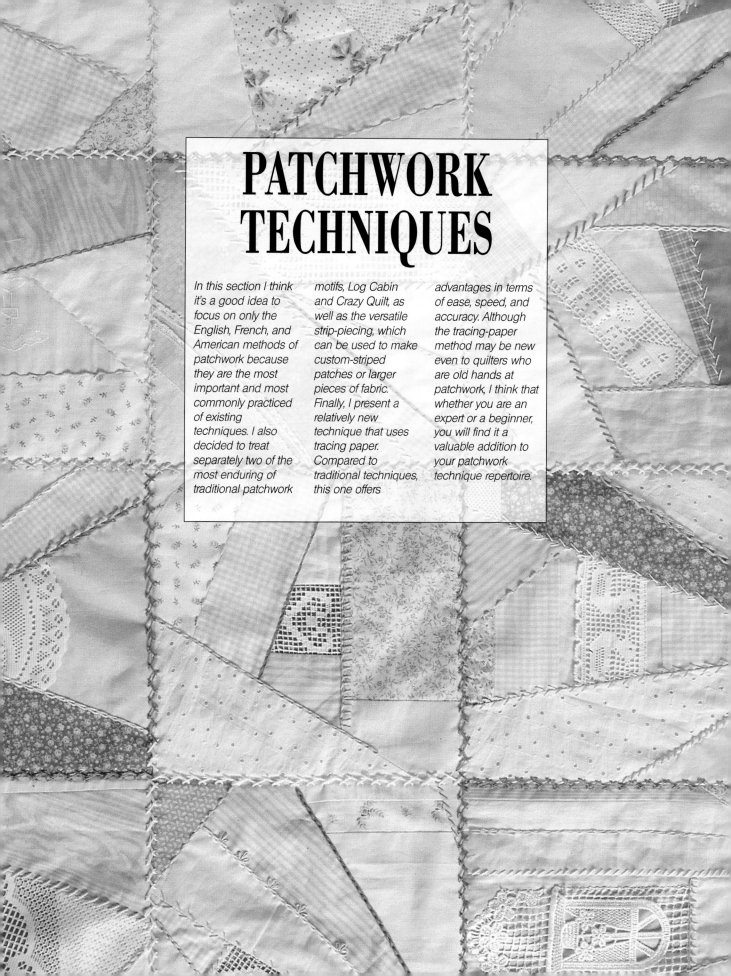

PATCHWORK TECHNIQUES

In this section I think it's a good idea to focus on only the English, French, and American methods of patchwork because they are the most important and most commonly practiced of existing techniques. I also decided to treat separately two of the most enduring of traditional patchwork motifs, Log Cabin and Crazy Quilt, as well as the versatile strip-piecing, which can be used to make custom-striped patches or larger pieces of fabric. Finally, I present a relatively new technique that uses tracing paper. Compared to traditional techniques, this one offers advantages in terms of ease, speed, and accuracy. Although the tracing-paper method may be new even to quilters who are old hands at patchwork, I think that whether you are an expert or a beginner, you will find it a valuable addition to your patchwork technique repertoire.

ENGLISH METHOD

In this mini-quilt of pieced hexagons, opposite, the center was made using the English method and the borders were made using the American method. (G. Berti)

The English method of piecing is most commonly used for small noncurved patchwork shapes. Work as follows:
- Draw two basic templates (A, B) on cardboard and then cut them out.
- Use the larger template (A), complete with seam allowance, to cut out the fabric patches; use the smaller template (B), the size of the finished patch, to cut the paper template.
- Pin a paper template to the center of each corresponding fabric patch, fold the seam allowance over the paper, baste, and press.
- Lay one of the prepared patches over another, right sides together, and hand-sew one edge with small, regular whip-stitching, without stitching through the paper. I recommend adding two secure anchoring stitches at each end of the seam.
- Join the other patches in the same way, do the final pressing, then remove all the basting.

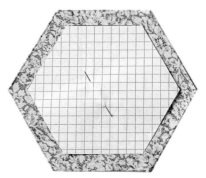

A template pinned onto a patch

A patch with edges folded in and basted

Two patches whip-stitched together

FRENCH METHOD

Paper template at the center of a fabric patch

The French method of piecing, known as appliqué, is mainly used for stitching curved or irregularly shaped fabric pieces onto a ground fabric. To hand-appliqué, work as follows:
- Draw two basic templates (A, B) on cardboard and then cut them out.
- Use the larger template (A), complete with seam allowance, to cut out the shaped fabric pieces; use the smaller template (B), the size of the finished shape, to cut out the paper template.
- Pin the paper template to the center of the fabric patch, fold the seam allowance over the paper, baste, and press.
Wherever a curve is concave, make a few cuts into the seam allowance so that it folds over more easily. Wherever a curve is convex, start with a running stitch along the seam line; pulling one of the thread ends will cause the seam to pucker, shaping it perfectly if the tension is just right.

- Press the appliqué, remove the basting and paper, then position the fabric shape on the ground fabric, baste, neatly blind-stitch, and remove the basting.
To machine-appliqué, use the smaller template (B) to cut a same-size fabric shape, minus seam allowance.
- Pin the fabric shape to the ground fabric, baste, zigzag-stitch by machine over the shaped edges, and remove the basting. Depending upon the fabrics used for the shaped pieces and ground, it may be helpful to add behind the ground fabric a thin backing that can be trimmed away after the appliqué is stitched in place. Using this additional layer will give a greater stability to your work, especially during stitching, sewing, washing, and pressing. If the appliqué motif is made of more than one fabric piece, layer the shapes as appropriate and stitch them in place in order,

working from the bottom layers upward. Using fusible-web tape makes appliqué a lot easier. A very thin layer of synthetic material, it is protected on both front and back by backing paper that is pulled off and removed before applying the tape. Fusible web leaves no visible marks and won't damage your fabric when it is being washed or pressed. Actually, it offers a number of advantages:
- it makes basting unnecessary;
- it adds stability to the finished piece without the need for an additional layer behind the ground;
- it eliminates the need to add or turn under seam allowance when doing hand – or machine – appliqué. In fact, this synthetic material, which dissolves during work from the heat of an iron, prevents the appliqué from fraying through washing or normal wear.

Folded and basted seam allowance

A template blind-stitched onto the ground material

This durable, washable book for Baby is made of softly padded fabric. It is decorated with appliquéd shapes sewn on by hand. (G. Berti)

AMERICAN METHOD

This geometric design, opposite, is set off by the interplay of colors and shades. (Coin)

In the American method, patches are placed together and stitched, right sides facing, either by hand or machine. This method is usually reserved for rectilinear designs and there are different ways of doing it. The following are the most popular:
- the traditional method, which uses paper templates and the marking of fabric;
- the Quick & Easy method, which uses a rotary cutter;
- the tracing-paper method, which is discussed later in this section.

THE TRADITIONAL METHOD

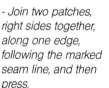

- Draw two basic templates (A, B) on cardboard and then cut them out.
- Use the larger template (A), complete with seam allowance, to cut out the fabric patches; use the smaller template (B), the size of the finished shape, to cut out the paper template.
- Pin each paper template onto the corresponding fabric patch and pencil-mark the seam allowance on the wrong side of the fabric.

- Join two patches, right sides together, along one edge, following the marked seam line, and then press.
- Join all patches the same way.

THE QUICK & EASY METHOD

The Quick & Easy method is quicker, easier, and more accurate than more traditional methods because it uses a rotary cutter instead of scissors.
This method eliminates the need to mark the fabric and enables the quiltmaker to cut many perfectly shaped patches in a short amount of time. Assembly-line stitching further speeds up the process.

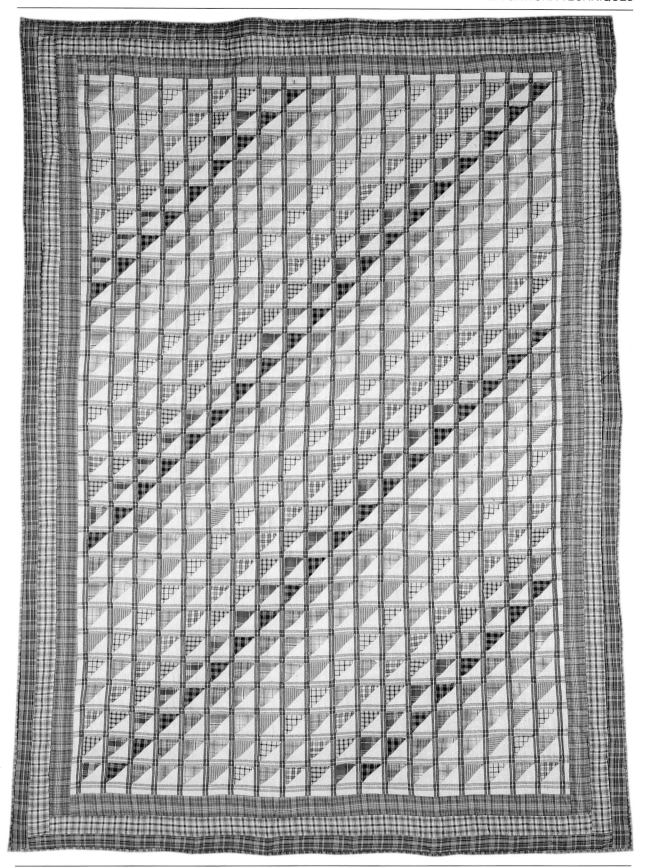

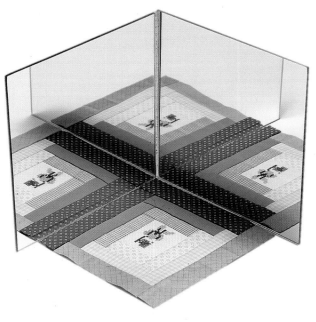

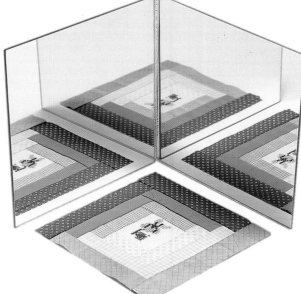

Mirrors show the effect of Log Cabin blocks joined with and without lattice.

LOG CABIN

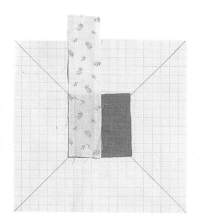

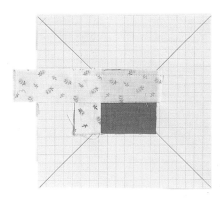

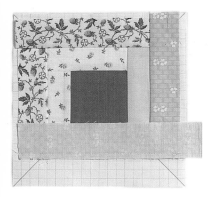

There are three ways of working Log Cabin patchwork:
- on a fabric ground, to add stability; (a check fabric can double as a guide for positioning patches horizontally and vertically);
- on graph paper, which is removed after the block is complete;
- with no base at all.

FABRIC-GROUND METHOD
(also useful for the other two methods)
- Cut a backing square from the ground fabric, then mark its diagonals on the right side.
- Cut out the fabric patches.
- Place patch 1, right side up, in the center of the backing square, then place a strip (patch 2), wrong side up, over patch 1.
- Stitch one edge, turn

over patch 2, and press flat.
- Along the adjacent (clockwise) edge of patches 1 and 2, pin, stitch, turn, and press patch 3.
- Along the adjacent (clockwise) edge of patches 2 and 3, pin, stitch, turn, and press patch 4.
Continue working in a clockwise manner until the ground is covered. To speed up the process, instead of cutting each strip to length before stitching, cut long strips from the desired fabric beforehand, then trim them as needed after stitching, as shown in the photos at left.

*A petite apron bib with
a Log Cabin motif.
(G. Berti)*

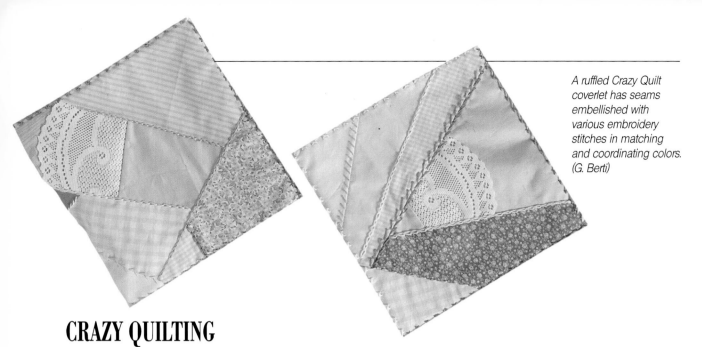

A ruffled Crazy Quilt coverlet has seams embellished with various embroidery stitches in matching and coordinating colors. (G. Berti)

CRAZY QUILTING

This method is reminiscent of early patchwork made from scraps of leftover fabric. Crazy Quilt is very easy to work and can be made to form interesting patterns with a little planning. The patchwork is made on a fabric ground, which adds stability, especially when using several weights of fabric scraps.

A Crazy Quilt for Baby can be attractively finished by embroidering over the seams and decorated by sewing tiny ribbons onto the quilt top. You can also use print fabrics with identifiable motifs that Baby might enjoy spotting.

There are several ways of working Crazy Quilt patchwork:
- place the first patch in the center or in a corner of the fabric ground;
- apply patches to a single piece of fabric the size of the entire quilt top;
- apply patches to several blocks, then join the blocks to form the quilt top.

Below are the directions for the multiple-block method (also useful for the other two methods):
- Cut out a block from the ground fabric.
- Pin the first patch, right side up, in one corner of the block. Place a second patch, wrong side up, over the first; stitch one edge, turn the second patch over, and press the seam flat; trim if necessary.
- Pin a third patch to one edge of the first two patches, stitch, press, and trim.
- Continue adding patches in this way until the ground is covered.
- Press the finished block and trim the edges.
- Make additional blocks, join them to make the quilt top, press, and trim.

In order to make the construction easier, be sure that the first patch, if placed in the center of the block, has more than four edges or, if placed in the corner, more than three. To speed up the process, you can cut patches made of strip-pieced fabric.

If two adjacent edges won't form a straight line, turn under the protruding patch and stitch it on the right side. Embroidery will cover this irregular seam, which will appear to be a planned design element and just make your Crazy Quilt even crazier.

STRIP-PIECING

It is very easy to work with strip-pieced fabric and the effects are both varied and eye-catching, especially when the fabric serves as a ground or border. Any type of strip will do:
- cut straight or on an angle; of the same or different widths, placed straight or on a slight angle;
- strips made of various other patches;
- with matching, contrasting, or random colors.

To conserve fabric, cut all the strips about the same width but not too narrow. From the strip-pieced fabric all kinds of motifs (flowers, food, animals, geometric shapes, etc.) can be cut and then appliquéd by hand or machine. Motifs can be carried out in both plain and patterned fabrics, greatly increasing the design options. Strip-pieced fabric is particularly attractive as a border.

A tablemat worked in the American style, with a central hexagon motif and strip-pieced border.

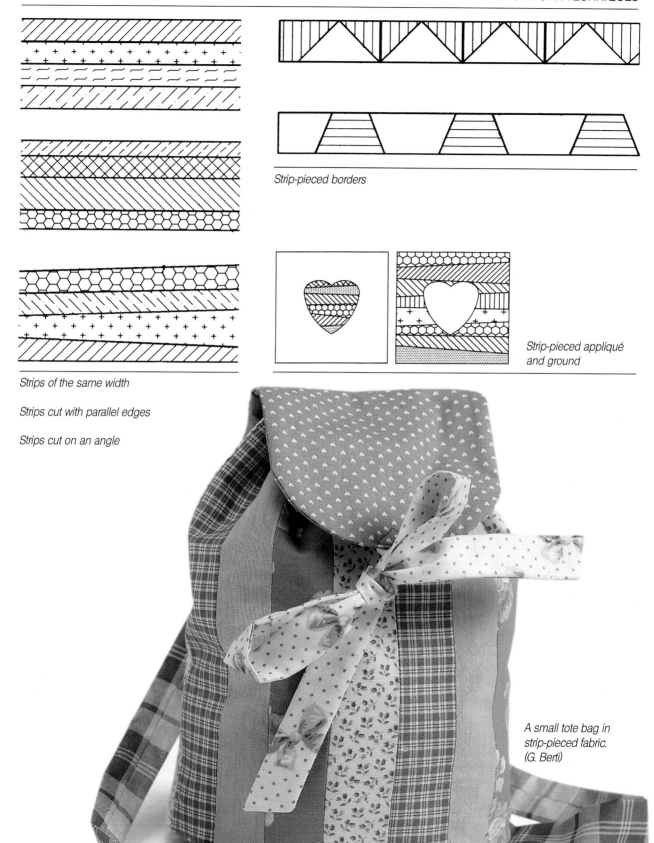

Strip-pieced borders

Strip-pieced appliqué
and ground

Strips of the same width

Strips cut with parallel edges

Strips cut on an angle

A small tote bag in
strip-pieced fabric.
(G. Berti)

TRACING-PAPER METHOD

I consider this method innovative because, although using paper to facilitate patchwork sewing is not new, using tracing paper is. You apply the fabric to one side of the paper and stitch on the

opposite side, which gives great precision. And precision, as those who have already make large patchwork pieces already know, is of the essence, particularly when there are

numerous seams to be matched.
The tracing-paper method is most suited for noncurved patches, for which it gives perfect results and takes much less time than traditional

techniques. Compared with the English method, it is a great time saver, and it beats the American one for precision. The most suitable type of tracing paper is that used for technical

drawing, also called acetate. It has just the right consistency and transparency, and it is easy to tear away when work is finished. As in all methods, cutting and stitching are the basic stages.

Different shaped patches worked in the tracing-paper method.

CUTTING

There are two methods of cutting. Method 1 is recommended for one or two patches. Method 2 is recommended when there are a large number of patches to be worked in series.

METHOD 1
- To make templates, draw your patchwork design on tracing paper, label the pieces, then cut them out.
- Pin the templates onto their corresponding pieces of fabric and cut out the patches, including seam allowance.

METHOD 2
- Draw your patchwork design on tracing paper, label the pieces, then place them on the desired fabric and cut them out using a rotary cutter. This is the Quick & Easy method, which involves cutting the strips beforehand and then cutting the patches in series. If you are a beginner to this technique, be sure to leave more seam allowance than actually needed, because excess fabric might come in handy if you need to make some changes; otherwise, the excess can be trimmed away.

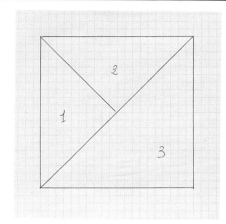
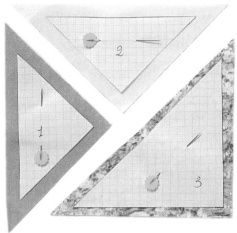
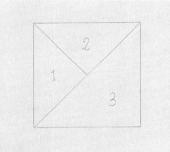

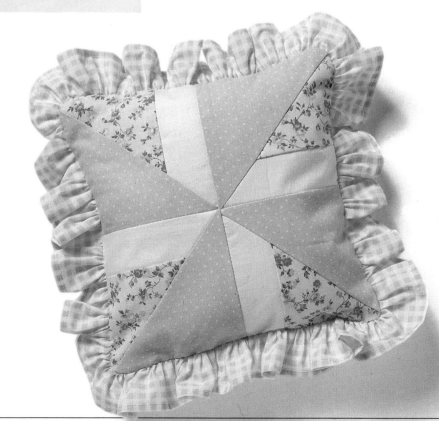

STITCHING

Work as follows:

- Choose a patchwork design from a book or magazine, or draw one actual size on graph paper; position the design on your work table, place a sheet of tracing paper over it, trace the design, and label each of the pieces.

- Place patch 2, right side up, on your work table, place patch 1, wrong side up, on top of patch 2, and lay the tracing paper over them, making sure it is perfectly aligned.

- Pin all three layers together, positioning the pins parallel to the seam line.

- Machine-stitch the edge where the patches are to be joined, starting a little before and ending a little after the seam.

- Lift the presser foot, remove the paper, trim the thread ends, and remove the pins.

- Turn over patch 2 and press the seam flat.

- Place patch 3, right side up, on your work table, place the tracing paper over it, pin, stitch, turn, and press.

- Continue adding patches in numerical order until the patchwork is complete.

- After stitching together all of the patches, tear off the paper, press and trim the borders of the block with a craft knife and a transparent quilting square. Pay particular attention when assembling asymmetrical patchwork designs, because the stitching

is done from the wrong side of the block whereas the motif appears reversed on the right side of the block. (Make sure that pieces that should extend to the left on the front of the work extend to the right on the back of the work.)

You can use the tracing-paper method to create most kinds of patchwork designs, including the traditional Log Cabin, Pineapple, Fence, Star, Pinwheel, and so on. With this method some designs will have to be worked in two or more sections. In the grid system used in this book, a dot on the line indicates where sections of a design are joined together.

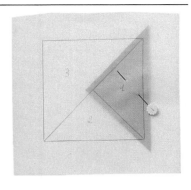

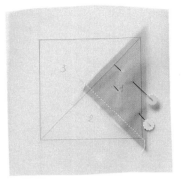

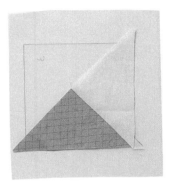

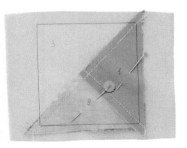

San Gallo and Valencienne laces soften the geometric composition of safety pin cushions (G. Berti)

MULTISECTION DESIGNS

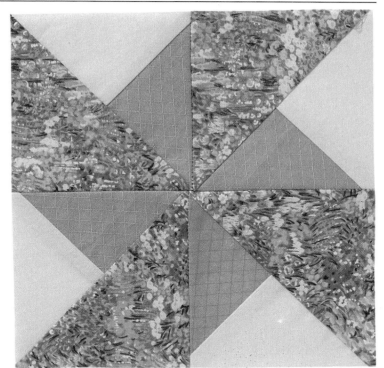

Work as follows:

- Draw your patchwork design on any kind of paper, then mark the lines dividing the sections.
- Reproduce each section on a separate sheet of tracing paper and label the pieces.
- Cut out the fabric patches.
- Pin, stitch, and press the patches of the first section, then those of the second and any additional sections.
- Sew the sections of the design together, press and trim the block with a craft knife and a quilting square. If you are a beginner to this technique, work at first with designs that:
- have stitching sequences already numbered;
- are simple and made up of few patches;
- preferably have parallel and perpendicular − not oblique − sewing lines;
- have only one section;
- are symmetrical. Only when you feel comfortable with this technique should you attempt more complicated designs. You can purchase quilting designs printed on special transfer paper, so called because the designs can be transferred with a hot iron directly onto the quilt top. The markings remain on the quilt, eliminating the need for stitching through paper and then removing it after quilting is complete. At this point, your quilt is just about complete. So to all of you quiltmakers out there, remember to enjoy your work and to put lots of love into it!

This pretty little bolster is decorated with an Ohio Star. (G. Berti)

PATCHWORK DESIGNS

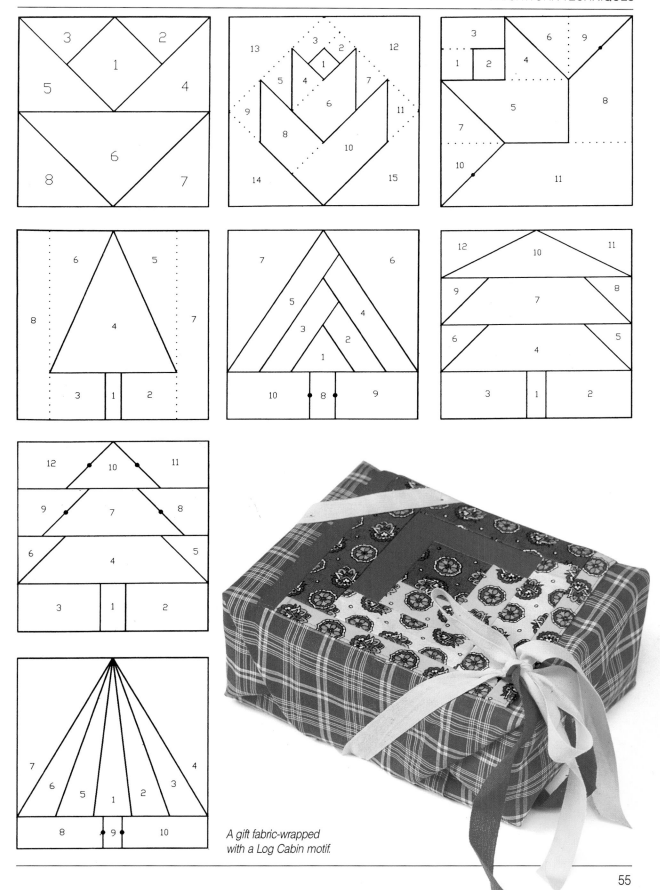

A gift fabric-wrapped with a Log Cabin motif.

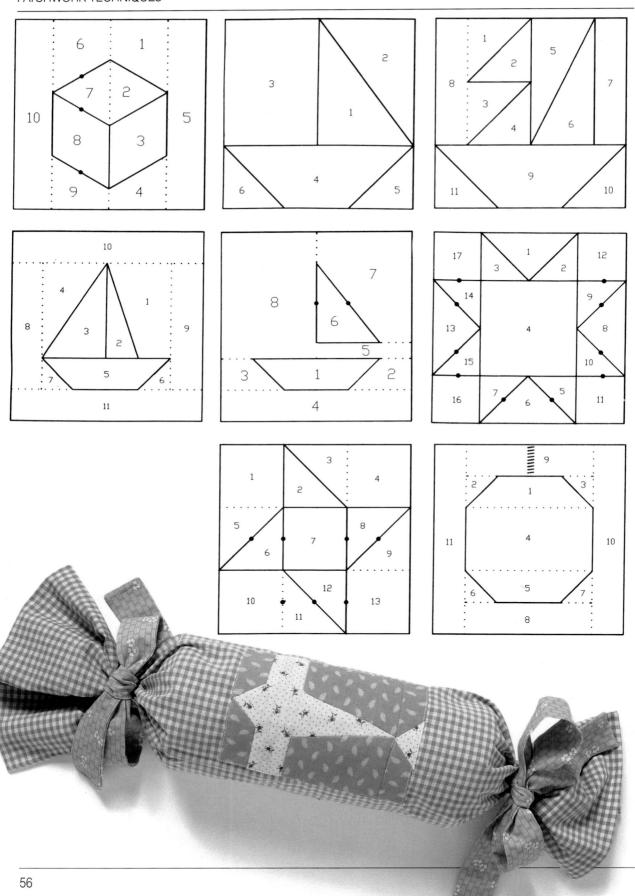

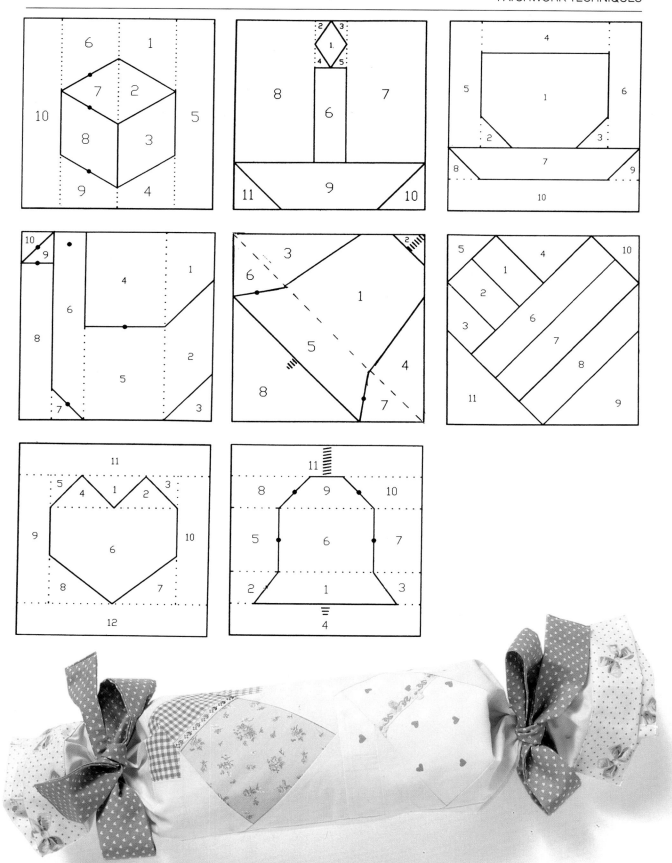

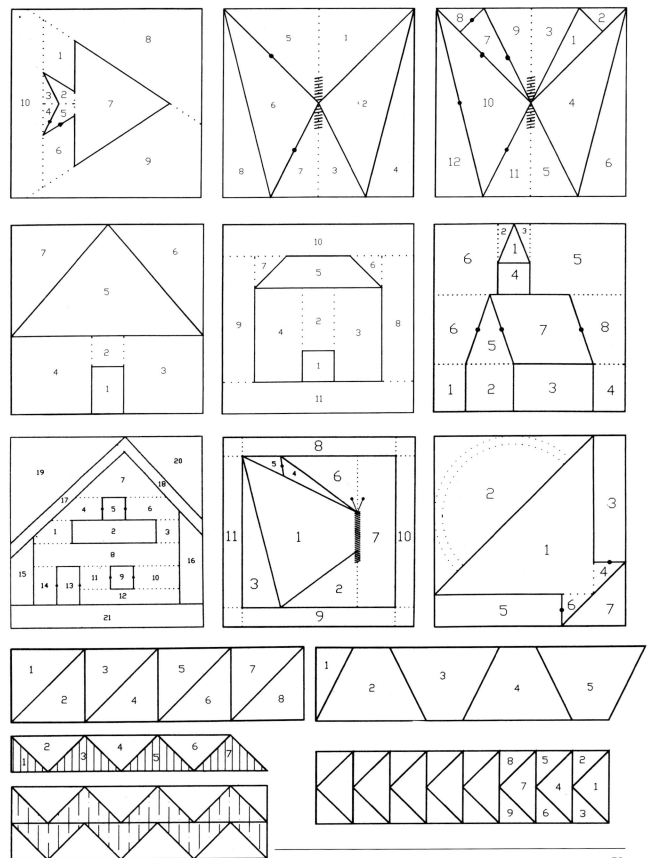

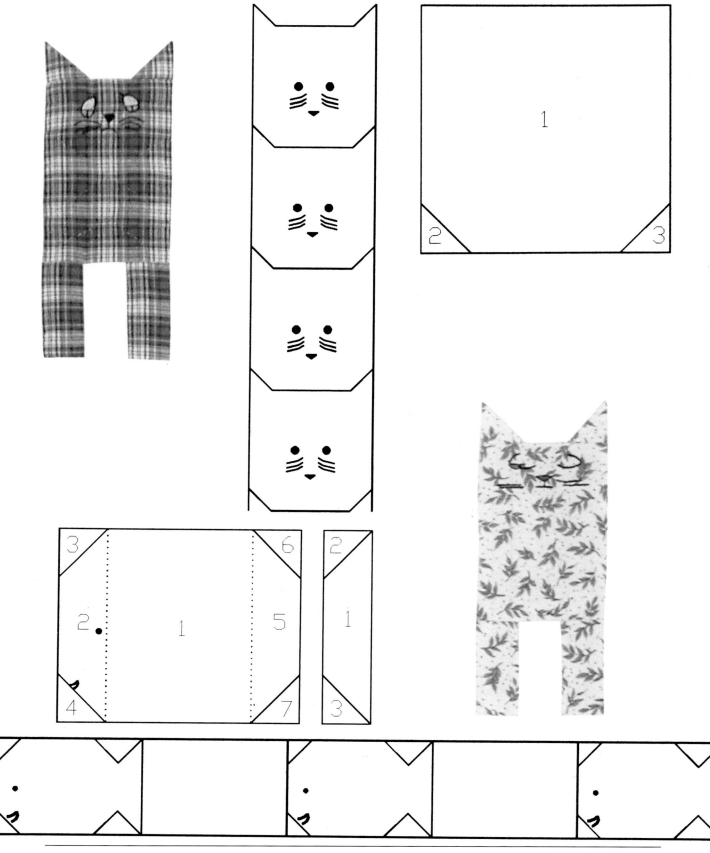

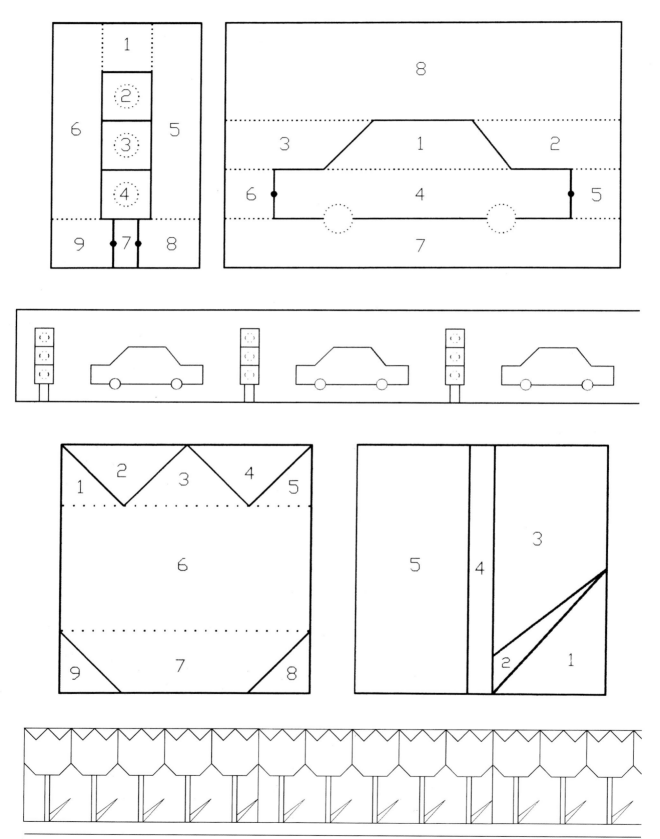

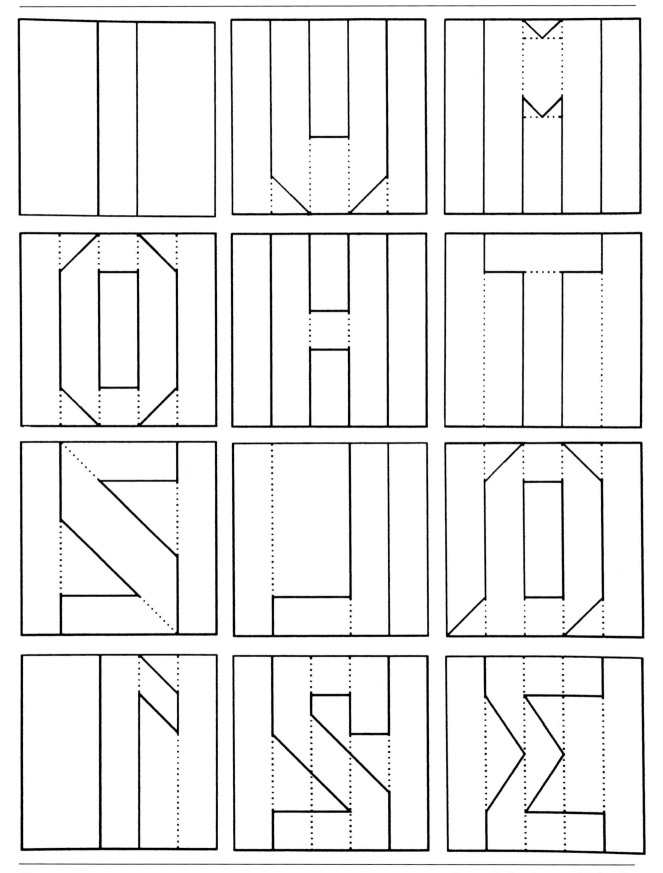

Symmetrical and asymmetrical motifs.

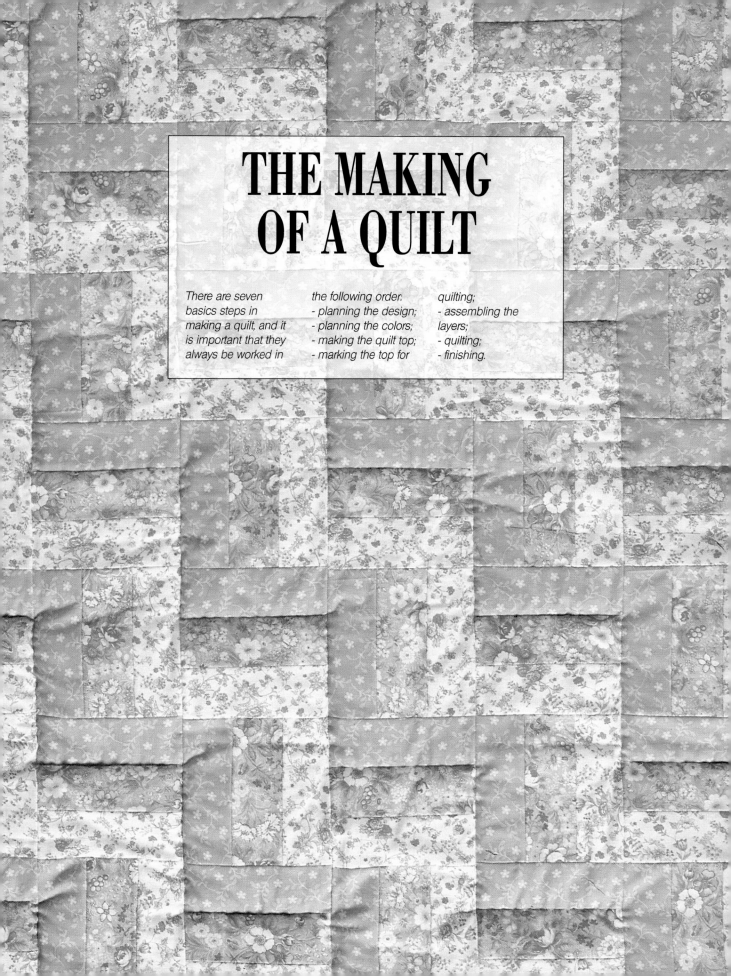

THE MAKING OF A QUILT

There are seven basics steps in making a quilt, and it is important that they always be worked in the following order:
- planning the design;
- planning the colors;
- making the quilt top;
- marking the top for quilting;
- assembling the layers;
- quilting;
- finishing.

PLANNING THE DESIGN

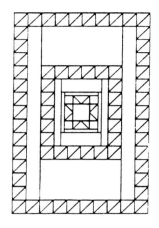

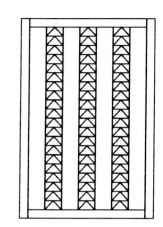

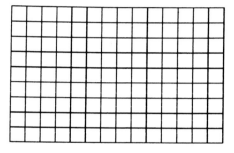
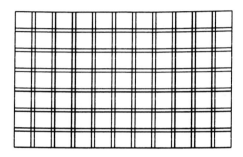

Those of you who are
newcomers to
patchwork might want
to consider buying a
prepared kit that
includes the fabric,
patterns, and complete
instructions for making
a quilt top. If you are
an experienced quilter,
you might want to
make a design of your
own creation.
The blocks could be
oriented parallel to the
quilt edges or on point
(at a 45-degree angle),
with or without strips of
lattice between them,
and with or without
one or more plain or
pieced borders.
Be sure to draft the
patchwork design on
graph paper, and mark
all of the dimensions
and any special
notations on it, such as
an embellishment
you want to remember
to add.

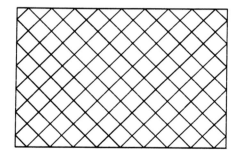
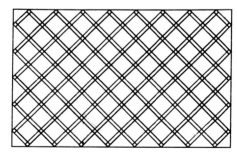

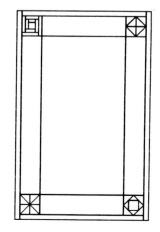
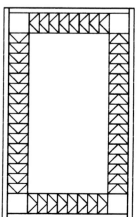

PLANNING THE COLORS

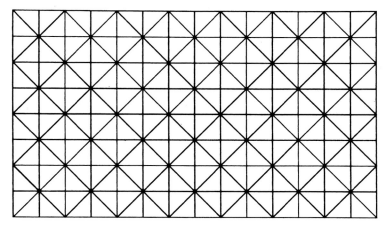

In order to plan your project's colors, start with a schematic or draft of the quilt top drawn on graph paper. You might want to have several photocopies of it made so that you can test different color combinations.
Try combinations of warm, cool, strong, subtle, light, and dark shades. Play with combinations of patterned and plain fabric until you are pleased with the result.
When wishing to achieve shaded tints, a chromatic filter is of great use. When placed on the different fabrics, it cancels the colors and emphasizes instead the graded values on the light/dark scale.

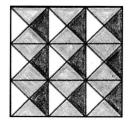
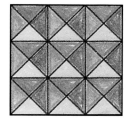
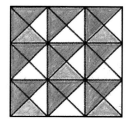

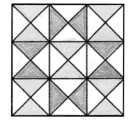

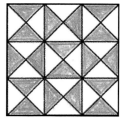

A chromatic filter, which cancels the fabric colors and emphasizes the bright/dark scale of values.

MAKING THE QUILT TOP

To make the top, various elements must first be cut out and then joined together in a logical sequence:
- in a design with a central motif, join the outer patches to the inner one(s), working from the center outward;
- in a design with squares, join these and any lattice together to form horizontal rows and then vertical columns;
- in a design with strips or bands, prepare the individual bands and then join them together;
- add the inner border, joining the horizontal members and the vertical ones;
- add any additional borders in the same manner;
- always press before proceeding to the next step.

Simple, easy-to-recognize figures are appliquéd to the blocks of this panel. (I. Wieland)

A central-motif composition

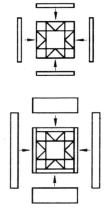

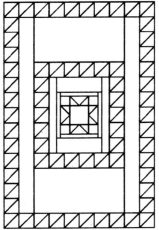

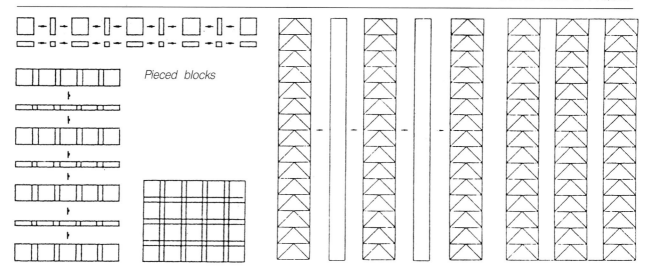

Pieced blocks

Pieced bands

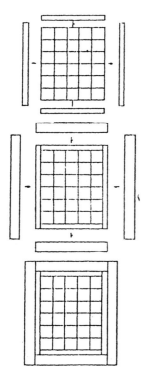

Joining the borders

Different shapes and sizes of blocks make up the center of this panel that features appliqués and lattice. (I. Wieland)

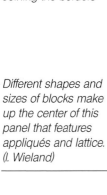

MARKING THE TOP FOR QUILTING

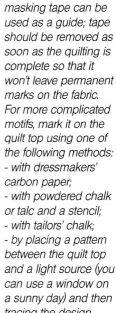

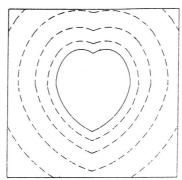

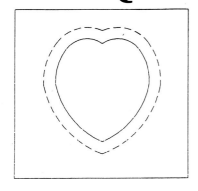

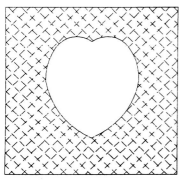

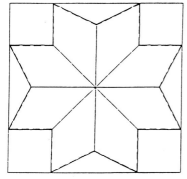

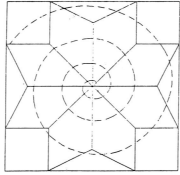

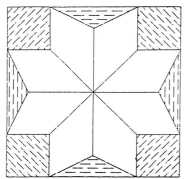

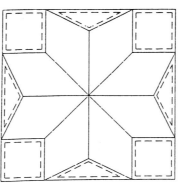

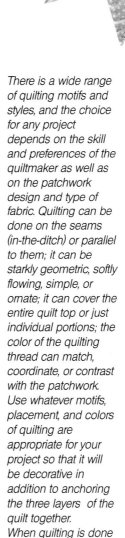

There is a wide range of quilting motifs and styles, and the choice for any project depends on the skill and preferences of the quiltmaker as well as on the patchwork design and type of fabric. Quilting can be done on the seams (in-the-ditch) or parallel to them; it can be starkly geometric, softly flowing, simple, or ornate; it can cover the entire quilt top or just individual portions; the color of the quilting thread can match, coordinate, or contrast with the patchwork. Use whatever motifs, placement, and colors of quilting are appropriate for your project so that it will be decorative in addition to anchoring the three layers of the quilt together.

When quilting is done along the seams, no marking of the quilt top is needed. When quilting consists of straight lines, the seams themselves or masking tape can be used as a guide; tape should be removed as soon as the quilting is complete so that it won't leave permanent marks on the fabric. For more complicated motifs, mark it on the quilt top using one of the following methods:

- with dressmakers' carbon paper;
- with powdered chalk or talc and a stencil;
- with tailors' chalk;
- by placing a pattern between the quilt top and a light source (you can use a window on a sunny day) and then tracing the design onto the right side of the fabric;
- by marking or tracing the quilting motif with tailor's chalk or a disappearing-ink marker specifically made for patchwork;
- for particularly complex drawings, use precut stencils; usually made of plastic, they can be purchased in a wide range of motifs and sizes.

Classic quilting motifs

*Quilting stencil with a
shell motif*

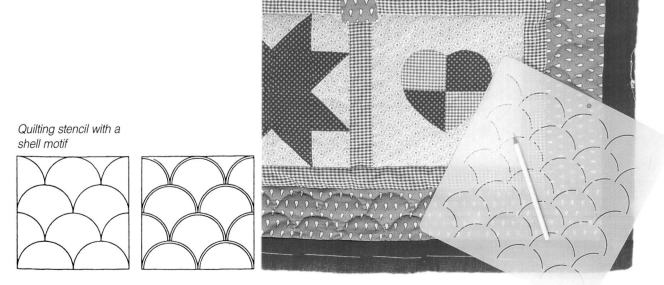

ASSEMBLING THE LAYERS

To layer the quilt, first place the backing, wrong side up, on a work table or floor. Then work as follows:
- secure the backing in place temporarily with tape;
- place the batting on top of the backing,

aligning the edges;
- baste the batting and backing together by making a giant cross-stitch in the center;
- center the quilt top over the batting, then pin and baste through all three layers completely across the

center of the quilt horizontally, vertically, and diagonally in both directions.
To speed up this part of the process, you can use safety pins or a tacking gun instead of basting stitches.

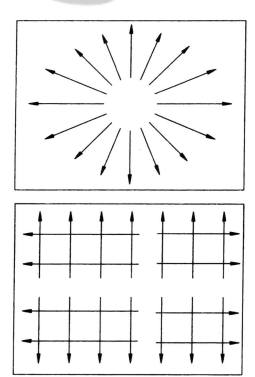

Tacking gun

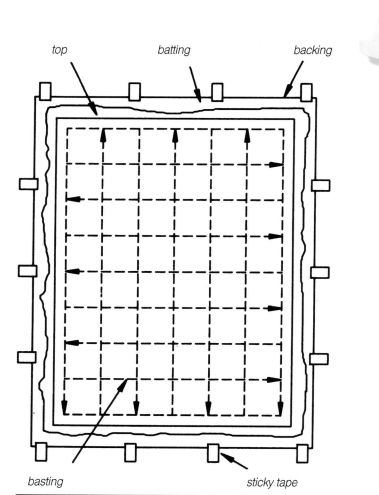

top   batting   backing

basting   sticky tape

Variations on the basting method

QUILTING

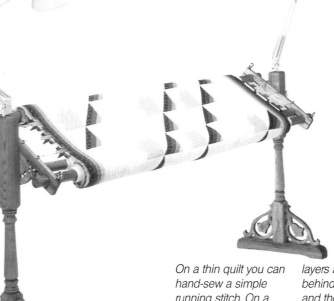

On a thin quilt you can hand-sew a simple running stitch. On a thicker quilt you can use the stab-stitch method, which is done in two steps: First the needle is inserted downward through the layers and pulled out behind the backing, and then it is inserted up through the layers and pulled out again on the front.

Short, fine needles give the best results. If you don't have quilting thread, which is particularly smooth and strong, you can substitute ordinary sewing thread if you double it. Quilting in a hoop or frame may not be necessary for small, fairly thin projects, but it is essential for large or thick ones.

To begin a thread, insert the needle from behind the piece and pull it through to the front until a knot that has been tied at the end is embedded in the batting. To end off a thread, knot it on the front of the quilt and thread it through to the back, embedding the knot in the batting. Although quilting has traditionally been done by hand, it can also be done by machine.

Quilting hoops and frames: round with adjustable rims and square with adjustable sides.

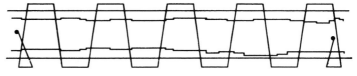

A side view of quilting stitches, including knots

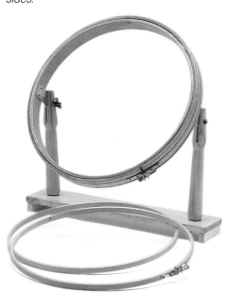

FINISHING

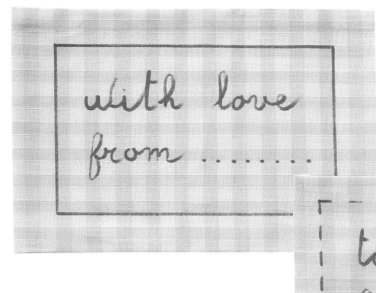

After the quilt top is complete, the outer edges of your project need to be bound. There are several ways of binding them, including the following:
- fold the edges of the quilt top to the wrong side and blind-stitch them to the backing;
- fold the edges of the backing to the front and blind-stitch them to the quilt top;
- turn in the edges of the quilt top and backing and then edge-stitch them together by hand or machine;
- finish the edges with separate strips of binding.

Remember to sign and date your quilt, whether you embroider it or write on the back with a permanent fine-tipped marker. You can also purchase fabric labels or make your own custom-designed ones, and add a greeting if you'd like. If you want to hang your quilt on a wall, stitch a tubular fabric sleeve to the top edge of the quilt through which a dowel can be inserted. If the quilt is fairly large and heavy, you might want to use a sturdy drapery pole to support it instead. Mount the dowel or pole on the wall following the manufacturer's directions or as desired.

Handmade check-fabric labels marked with permanent ink.

A whimsical wrought-iron hanger supports this charming appliquéd coverlet.

THE PROJECTS

In the directions in this book, all of the measurements given are finished size, so be sure to add appropriate seam allowance, usually 1/4" (0.6 cm) for patchwork. Different techniques were used to make the various projects, and the technique for each is specified, but you can use whichever method works best for you. Before beginning a quilt top made of identical blocks, make a sample first – you can always turn the sample into a pincushion, pillow, potholder, or wall hanging.

HAPPY QUILTING!!

DUCKLINGS

MATERIALS

- light blue and white fabrics for blocks and borders
- yellow fabric for pieced border
- dark blue fabric for outer border
- white Aida cloth
- embroidery floss
- fusible web
- batting
- backing

SIZE
block: 6 ¹/₂" (16 cm) square
finished piece: 30 ³/₄" x 37 ¹/₄" (77 x 93 cm)

TECHNIQUE
tracing paper

INSTRUCTIONS

- Back the Aida cloth with fusible web, cross-stitch the ducklings, then cut into 3 ¹/₄" (8 cm) squares.
- Draw, cut, and piece 6 ¹/₂" (16 cm) square duckling blocks.
- Cut 6 ¹/₂" (16 cm) square plain blocks.
- Join the plain and pieced blocks to form rows.
- Join the rows to form the 19 ¹/₂" x 26" (48 x 64 cm) quilt center.
- Press; remove the paper.
- Cut and join the 2" (5 cm) first border to the quilt center.
- For the sawtooth second border, cut 1 ¹/₂" - wide (3.75 cm) yellow and light blue strips.
- From the strips cut 1 ¹/₂" (3.75 cm) squares, then cut half-square triangles.
- Join the triangles in pairs to make squares.
- Join the squares to form border strips, then join the strips to the quilt top.
- Cut and join the 1 ¹/₂" (3.75 cm) third border to the quilt top.
- Cut the ¹/₂" (1.25 cm) outer border, adding 2" (5 cm) for finishing; join it to the quilt top.
- Cut the batting and backing 30 ³/₄" x 37 ¹/₄" (77 x 93 cm).
- Layer the backing, batting, and top; baste, then quilt.
- Finish the edges by folding the outer border over the backing; blind-stitch.

A label provides a personal touch.

G. Berti.

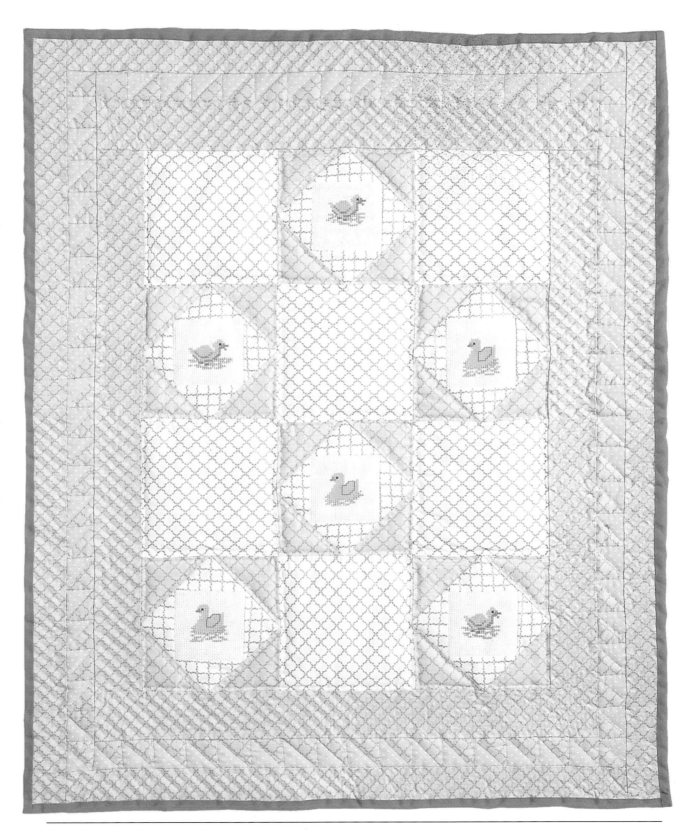

DRESSES

Facing is a coverlet by G. Berti from an idea in Quilt for Kids.

MATERIALS

- assorted fabrics for blocks
- pale pink fabric for background
- medium pink fabric for inner border
- dark pink fabric for middle border
- maroon fabric for outer border
- batting
- backing

SIZE
block: 6 ½" (16 cm) square
finished piece: 38" x 46 ¾" (96 x 117 cm)

TECHNIQUE
tracing paper

A small, bonbon-shaped bolster with a dresses motif. (G. Berti)

INSTRUCTIONS

- Draw, cut, and piece 6 ½" (16 cm) square dress blocks.
- Press; remove the paper.
- Sew ribbons or other desired trims onto the dresses.
- Cut 6 ½" (16 cm) squares and 6 ½" x 4 ½" (16 x 11 cm) right-angle triangles from the background fabric.
- Join the plain and pieced blocks and triangles to form rows.
- Join the rows to form the 26 ½" x 35 ¼" (66 x 88 cm) quilt top.
- Cut and join to the quilt top the 1 ¼" (3 cm) inner border, the 4" (10 cm) middle border, and the ½" (1.25 cm) outer border, adding 2" (5 cm) for finishing.
- Cut the batting and backing 38" x 46 ¾" (96 x 117 cm).
- Layer the backing, batting, and top; baste, then quilt.
- Finish the edges by folding the outer border over the backing; blind-stitch.

CABIN IN THE WOODS

MATERIALS

- assorted green fabric for trees and outer
  border
- brown fabric for tree trunks
- pale fabric for background
- red fabric for inner border and house accents
- pink fabric for house wall
- batting
- backing

SIZE
block: 6 $\frac{1}{2}$" (16 cm) square
finished piece: 27 $\frac{1}{2}$" x 34"
(68 x 84 cm)

TECHNIQUE
tracing paper

INSTRUCTIONS

- Draw, cut and piece 6 $\frac{1}{2}$" (16 cm) square pine tree and house blocks.
- Press; remove the paper.

- Join the blocks to form rows.
- Sew the rows vertically to make the 19 $\frac{1}{2}$" x 26" (48 x 64 cm) quilt top.
- Cut and join the $\frac{3}{4}$" (2 cm) inner border and the 3 $\frac{1}{4}$" (8 cm) outer border, adding 2" (5 cm) for finishing.
- Cut the batting and backing 27 $\frac{1}{2}$" x 34" (68 x 84 cm).
- Layer the backing, batting, and top; baste, then quilt.
- Finish the edges by folding the outer border over the backing; blind-stitch.

A block with a pine tree motif is used for wrapping a present. (G. Berti)

G. Berti from an idea
in Go Wild with Quilts.

VILLAGE

MATERIALS

- assorted fabrics for blocks and middle border
- medium green fabric for lattice and inner border
- dark green fabric for outer border
- batting
- backing

SIZE
block: 6" (15 cm) square
finished piece: 41 $\frac{1}{2}$" x 47 $\frac{1}{2}$" (103 x 120 cm)

TECHNIQUE
tracing paper

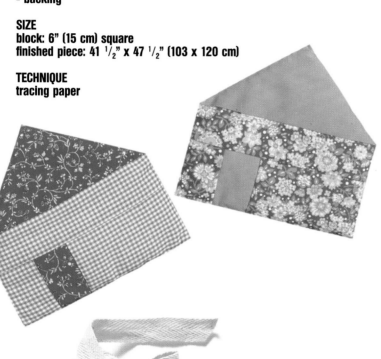

INSTRUCTIONS

- Draw, cut, and piece 6" (15 cm) square house blocks and 3" x 6" (7.5 cm x 15 cm) tree blocks.
- Join the square and rectangular blocks to form rows.
- Cut 1 $\frac{1}{2}$" (3.75 cm) lattice strips and join them between the pieced rows to make the 30" x 36" (75 x 90 cm) quilt center.
- Cut and join the 1 $\frac{1}{2}$" (3.75 cm) inner border to the quilt center.

- Cut and join the 3 $\frac{1}{4}$" (8 cm) strip-pieced middle border.
- Cut and join the $\frac{1}{2}$" (1.25 cm) outer border, adding 2" (5 cm) for finishing.
- Cut the batting and backing 41 $\frac{1}{2}$" x 47 $\frac{1}{2}$" (103 x 120 cm).
- Layer the backing, batting, and top; baste, then quilt.
- Finish the edges by folding the outer border over the backing; blind-stitch.

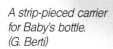

A strip-pieced carrier for Baby's bottle.
(G. Berti)

By G. Berti from an
idea in Miniature Quilts
(Sept. '95).

"BUONA NOTTE"

MATERIALS

- assorted green fabrics for blocks, hearts, and borders
- white Aida cloth
- embroidery floss
- fusible web
- batting
- backing

SIZE
block: 10" (25 cm) square
finished piece: 39" x 49" (98 x 122 cm)

TECHNIQUES
tracing paper and appliqué

Log Cabin blocks with
cross-stitched trees.
(G. Berti)

INSTRUCTIONS

- Back the Aida cloth with fusible web; cross-stitch the letters and bows, then cut into 4" (10 cm) squares.
- Draw, cut, and piece 10" (25 cm) square Log Cabin blocks, using 1" (2.5 cm) strips.
- Press; remove the paper.
- Join the blocks to make rows.
- Join the rows to make the 30" x 40" (75 x 100 cm) quilt center.
- Cut and join to the quilt center the $^1/_2$" (1.25 cm) inner border, the 3 $^1/_4$" (8 cm) middle border, and the $^3/_4$" (2 cm) outer border, adding 2" (5 cm) for finishing.
- Cut and appliqué hearts to the middle border.
- Cut the batting and backing 39" x 49" (98 x 122 cm).
- Layer the backing, batting, and top; baste, then quilt.
- Finish the edges by folding the outer border over the backing; blind-stitch.

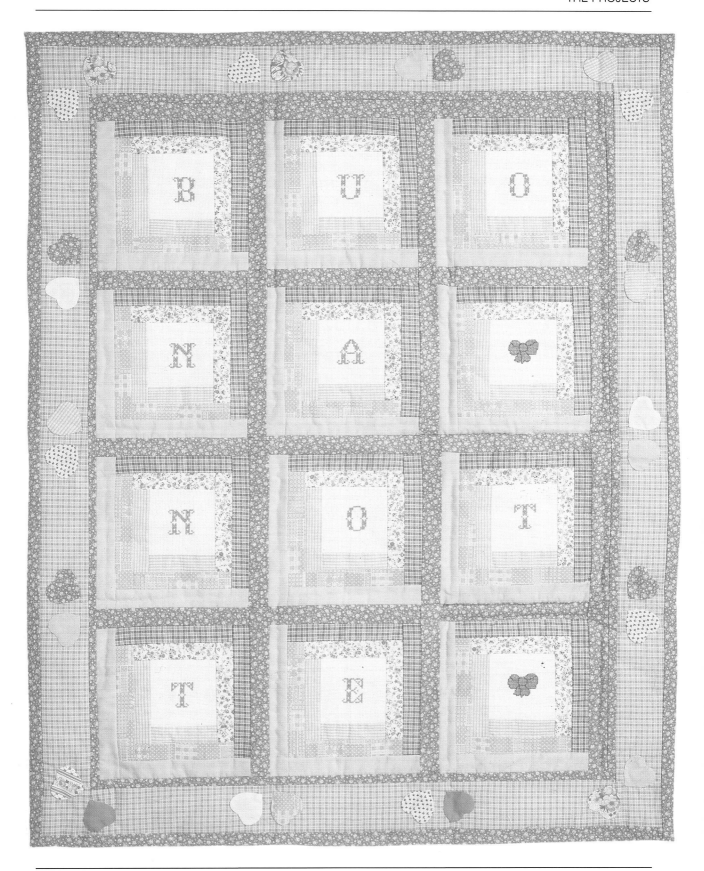

PINK HOUSES

MATERIALS

- assorted pink and green fabrics for blocks, lattice, and borders
- white Aida cloth
- embroidery floss, pink
- fusible web
- pink ribbon

SIZE
block: 6 ³/₄" (17 cm) square
finished piece: 24 ¹/₂" x 31 ¹/₄"
(61 x 78 cm)

TECHNIQUE
tracing paper

INSTRUCTIONS

This coverlet can be used year round if you remove the batting for warmer seasons and insert it for cooler ones.
- Back the Aida cloth with fusible web, cross-stitch the houses, then cut into 3 ¹/₄" (8 cm) squares.
- Draw, cut, and piece 6 ³/₄" (17 cm) square Log Cabin blocks, using ¹/₂" (1.5 cm) strips.
- Join the blocks to form rows.
- Join the rows to form the 20 ¹/₄" x 27" (51 x 68 cm) quilt center.
- Press; remove the paper.
- Cut and join to the quilt center the ³/₈" (1 cm) inner border and the 1 ⁵/₈" (4 cm) outer border.
- Cut the batting and backing 24 ¹/₂" x 31 ¹/₄" (61 x 78 cm).
- Layer the quilt top and batting; baste.
- Stitch the backing to the quilt top, right sides facing, leaving an opening in one edge for turning.
- Turn the quilt right side out; whip-stitch the opening closed. If the quilt will be a wallhanging, sew tiny ribbon bows to the bottom edge.

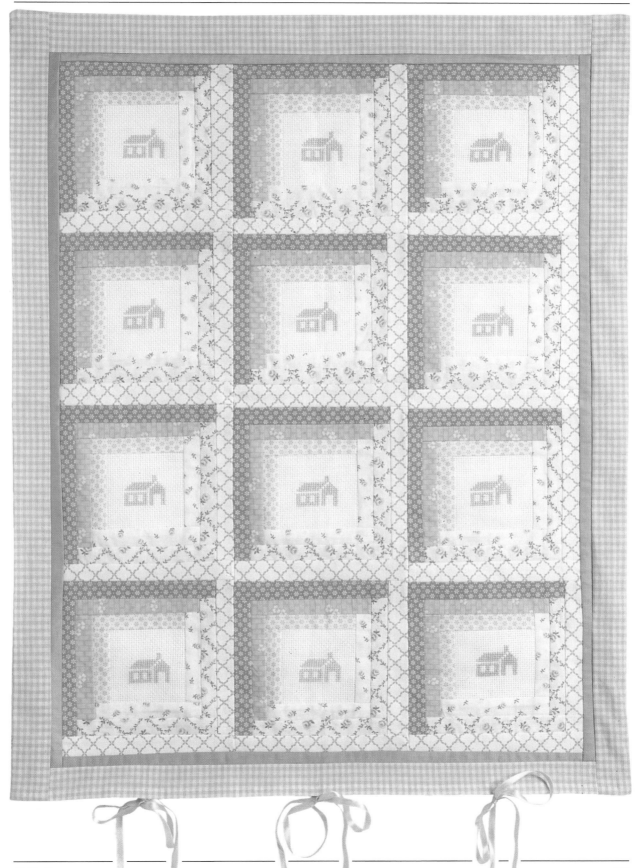

G. Berti

PINWHEELS

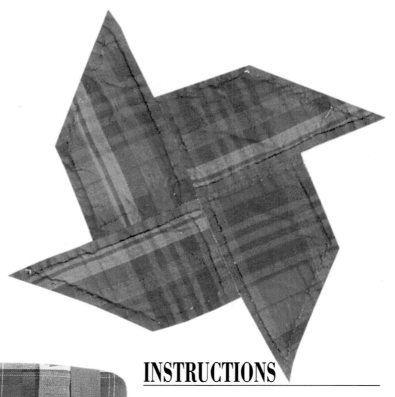

MATERIALS

- assorted plain and print fabrics
- ecru fabrics for background and border
- batting
- backing

SIZE
block: 5 $^1/_2$" (14 cm) square
finished piece: 41" x 57 $^1/_2$" (104 x 144 cm)

TECHNIQUES
tracing paper and appliqué

INSTRUCTIONS

- Make 5 $^1/_2$" (14 cm) square pinwheel blocks.
- Join the blocks to form rows.
- Join the rows to form the 33" x 49" (84 x 124 cm) quilt center.
- Press; remove the paper.
- Cut and join the 4" (10 cm) border, adding 2" (5 cm) for finishing.

- Mark the quilting motif on the border.
- Cut the batting and backing 41" x 57 $^1/_2$" (104 x 144 cm).
- Layer the backing, batting, and top; baste, then quilt.
- Finish the edges by folding the backing over the border; blind-stitch.

A lace ruffle adds a frilly touch to the patchwork square on this gift wrap. (G. Berti)

Coin

VIOLETS IN LOG CABINS

MATERIALS

- assorted pink and green fabrics for blocks, lattice, and borders
- white Aida cloth
- embroidery floss
- fusible web
- batting
- backing

SIZE
block: 7 $\frac{1}{4}$" (18 cm) square
finished piece: 36 $\frac{3}{4}$" x 29 $\frac{1}{2}$"
(92 x 74 cm)

TECHNIQUE
tracing paper

A cozy to keep Baby's food warm.
(A. Alessandri)

INSTRUCTIONS

- Cross-stitch the violets, then cut into 7 $\frac{1}{4}$" (18 cm) squares.
- Draw, cut, and piece 7 $\frac{1}{4}$" (18 cm) square Log Cabin blocks, using $\frac{7}{8}$" (2 cm) strips.
- Join the blocks to form rows.
- Join the rows to form the 29" x 21 $\frac{3}{4}$" (72 x 54 cm) quilt center.
- Press; remove the paper.
- Cut and join to the quilt center the 1" (2.5 cm) inner border, the 2 $\frac{1}{2}$" (6.3 cm) middle border, and the $\frac{3}{8}$" (1 cm) outer border, adding 2" (5 cm) for finishing.
- Cut the batting and backing 36 $\frac{3}{4}$" x 29 $\frac{1}{2}$" (92 x 74 cm).
- Layer the backing, batting, and top; baste, then quilt.
- Finish the edges.

*Parma Patchwork
Club.*

BUNNIES

MATERIALS

- ecru fabric for background and borders
- assorted light- and medium-blue fabrics for appliqués and inner border
- embroidery floss, green
- fusible web
- batting
- backing

SIZE
finished piece: 47" x 55 $\frac{3}{4}$" (116 x 138 cm)

TECHNIQUES
American method and appliqué

INSTRUCTIONS

- Cut the 34 $\frac{1}{2}$" x 43 $\frac{1}{4}$" (86 x 108 cm) background.
- Cut and appliqué the bunnies and carrots onto the background.
- Embroider the carrot leaves.

- For the sawtooth border, cut 2 $\frac{3}{8}$" (6 cm) strips.
- From the strips cut 2 $\frac{3}{8}$" (6 cm) squares, then cut half-square triangles.
- Join the triangles in pairs to make squares.
- Join the squares to form border strips, then join the strips to the quilt top.
- Cut and join to the quilt top the 2 $\frac{5}{8}$" (6 cm) middle border and the 1 $\frac{1}{4}$" (3 cm) outer border, adding 2" (5 cm) for finishing.
- Cut the batting and backing 47" x 55 $\frac{3}{4}$" (116 x 138 cm).
- Layer the backing, batting, and top; baste, then quilt.
- Finish the edges by folding the outer border over the backing; blind-stitch.

*Parma Patchwork
Club.*

SUE 'N' SAM

MATERIALS

- light-on-white print fabric for background
- assorted dark and bright fabrics for appliqués and backing
- batting
- red knit coverlet

SIZE
finished patchwork: 20" x 28" (50 x 70 cm)
finished piece: 22" x 30" (55 x 75 cm)

TECHNIQUE
appliqué

INSTRUCTIONS

This warm, cozy coverlet is particularly suited for outings in a stroller, but it works just as well in a baby carriage or crib all year round, because the patchwork center can be removed and used alone when the weather is warm.
- Cut the 20" x 28" (50 x 70 cm) background.
- Cut and appliqué the children onto the background.

- Cut the batting 22" x 30" (55 x 75 cm) and the backing 26" x 34" (65 x 85 cm).
- Layer the backing, batting, and top; baste, then quilt.
- Finish the edges by folding the backing over the background to form a binding; blind-stitch.
- Blind-stitch the quilt to a 44" x 32" (110 x 80 cm) knit coverlet.

Sun Bonnet Sue adorns this gift wrap and bib. (G. Berti)

CUPS AND SAUCERS

MATERIALS

- ecru fabric for block backgrounds
- dark green fabric for lattice and inner border
- assorted fabrics for appliqués, outer border, and "pinked" trim
- batting
- backing

SIZE
block: 6 ¹/₂" (16 cm) square
finished piece: 36 ⁵/₈" x 28 ³/₄" (92 x 72 cm) plus trim

TECHNIQUE
appliqué

INSTRUCTIONS

- Cut 6 ¹/₂" (16 cm) square blocks from the background fabric.
- Cut and appliqué the cups onto the blocks.
- Cut 1 ³/₈" (3.5 cm) lattice strips.
- Join the blocks and vertical lattice to form rows.
- Join the rows and horizontal lattice to form the 30 ¹/₈" x 22 ¹/₄" (76 x 56 cm) quilt center.
- Cut and join the 1 ¹/₄" (3.125 cm) inner border to the quilt center.
- Cut and join the 2" (5 cm) outer border to the quilt center.
- To make the triangles for the outer trim, cut 2 ¹/₂" (5 cm) strips, then 2 ¹/₂" (5 cm) squares.
- Fold the squares into 1 ¹/₄" (2.5 cm) half-square triangles.
- Stitch the triangles to the border; press the trim away from the border and the seam allowance toward the border.
- Cut the 36 ⁵/₈" x 28 ³/₄" (92 x 72 cm) batting and 37 ¹/₈" x 29 ¹/₄" (93 x 73 cm) backing.
- Layer the backing, batting, and top; baste, then quilt.
- Finish the edges by folding the backing to the inside, covering the triangle seams; blind-stitch.

TEDDY BEARS

MATERIALS

- pale pink fabric for background
- assorted pink and green fabrics for appliqués and borders
- batting
- backing
- polyester fiberfill for stuffing
- narrow pink ribbon

SIZE
finished piece: 37 ³/₄" x 49 ³/₄"
(95 x 125 cm)

TECHNIQUE
appliqué

INSTRUCTIONS

- Cut the 31 ¹/₄" x 43 ¹/₄" (78 x 108 cm) background.
- Cut out the teddy bears and basket handle, then appliqué them onto the background.
- Cut out the basket, then appliqué it in place below the handle, leaving an opening in the top edge for holding the stuffed teddy bear.
- Cut and join to the background the ¹/₂" (1.25 cm) inner border and the 2 ³/₄" (7 cm)

outer border, adding 2" (5 cm) for finishing.
- Cut the batting and backing 37 ³/₄" x 49 ³/₄" (95 x 125 cm).
- Mark the quilting design on the quilt center.
- Layer the backing, batting, and top; baste, then quilt.
- Finish the edges by folding the outer border over the backing; blind-stitch.
- Cut, stitch, turn, and stuff the basket bear; whip-stitch the opening closed.

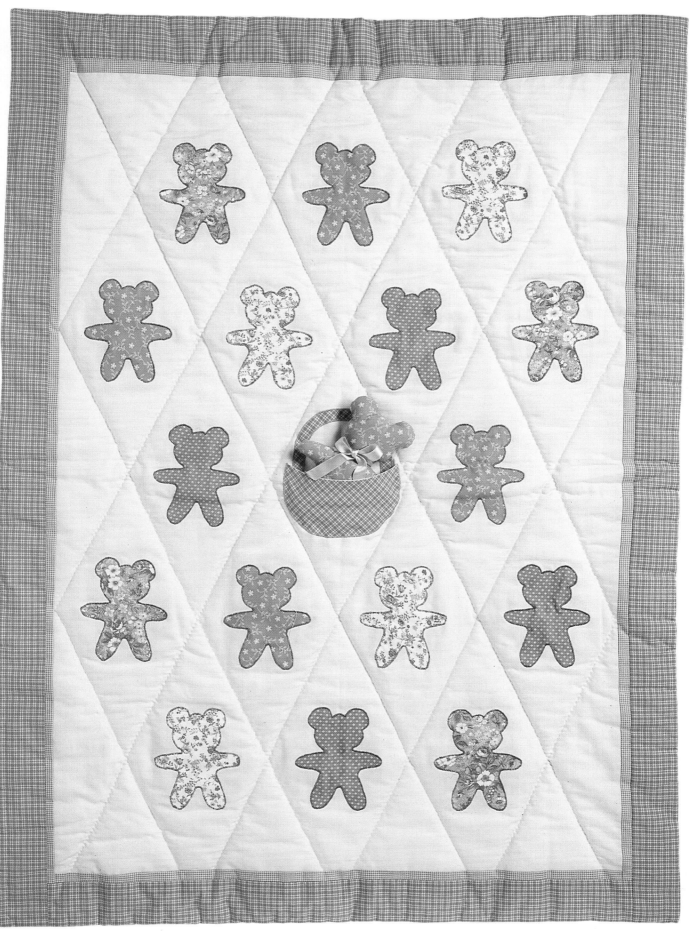

G. Berti

BABY BUGGIES

MATERIALS

- pale pink gingham fabric for background
- assorted pink fabrics for appliqués and border
- dark pink fabric for backing
- batting
- pale pink ribbon

SIZE
finished piece: 28 $^3/_4$" x 34 $^3/_4$" (72 x 87 cm)

TECHNIQUE
appliqué

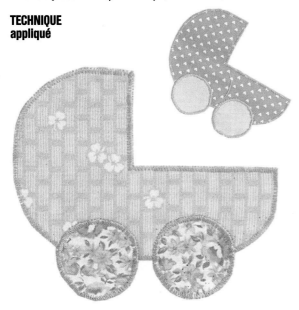

INSTRUCTIONS

- Cut the 24" x 30" (60 x 75 cm) background.
- Mark 6 $^3/_8$" (16 cm) on-point squares on the background.
- Cut out and appliqué the baby buggies to the background.
- Cut and sew on the 2 $^3/_8$" (6 cm) border.
- Cut the 28 $^3/_4$" x 34 $^3/_4$" (72 x 87 cm)

batting and 29 $^1/_2$" x 35 $^1/_4$" (74 x 88 cm) backing.
- Layer the backing, batting and top; baste, then quilt.
- Finish the edges by folding the backing over the border; blind-stitch.
- Sew two tiny ribbon bows to the quilt top.

LACE-TRIMMED BASSINET

This coverlet can be used all year long by inserting or removing batting.

MATERIALS

- **assorted pink fabrics for bassinet and border**
- **white fabric for background**
- **assorted blue fabrics for birds**
- **assorted green fabrics for leaves and border**
- **embroidery floss, yellow**
- **ruffled eyelet and flat slotted lace**
- **pale pink ribbons**
- **batting**
- **backing**

SIZE
quilt center: 14 ³/₄" x 13 ¹/₄" (37 x 33 cm)
finished piece: 24" x 29 ¹/₄" (60 x 73 cm)

TECHNIQUE
appliqué

INSTRUCTIONS

- *Cut the 10" x 8 ³/₈" (25 x 21 cm) quilt center.*
- *Cut out and appliqué the bassinet, birds, and leaves onto the quilt center.*
- *Stitch on the eyelet edging, then embroider the birds' beaks.*
- *Cut and join to the quilt center the 2 ³/₈" (6 cm) strip-pieced inner border.*

- *Cut the 24" x 29 ¹/₄" (60 x 73 cm) coverlet, then appliqué the patchwork onto it.*
- *Thread ribbon through the slotted lace, then stitch it around the strip-pieced border.*
- *Cut the batting and backing 24" x 29 ¹/₄" (60 x 73 cm).*
- *Layer the quilt top and batting; baste.*
- *Stitch the backing to*

the quilt top, right sides facing, leaving an opening in one edge for turning.
- *Turn the quilt right side out; whip-stitch the opening closed.*
- *Sew tiny ribbon bows to the upper left corner of the strip-pieced border.*
If the quilt will be a wallhanging, sew tiny ribbon bows to the bottom edge.

G. Berti

TREE SKIRT

This red and green appliquéd skirt with its ruffled outer edge would be a cheerful addition under any Christmas tree.

MATERIALS

- red fabric for background and ruffle
- assorted fabrics for appliqués
- narrow red ribbon

SIZE
finished piece:
40" (100 cm) diameter

TECHNIQUE
appliqué

INSTRUCTIONS

- Cut the round skirt with a 20" (50 cm) radius, back opening, and circular cutout at the center; hem the inner cut edges.
- Cut out and appliqué the shapes onto the skirt.
- Cut, prepare, and stitch the 2" (5 cm) ruffle to the outer edge of the skirt.
- Sew ribbons to the back opening for fasteners.

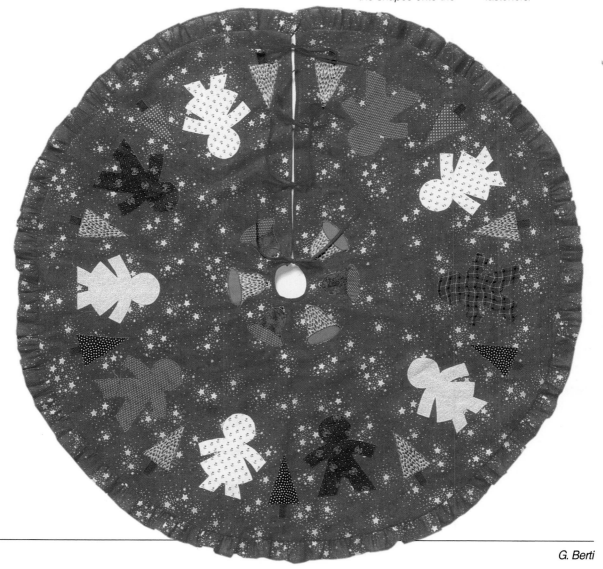

G. Berti

CLAMSHELLS

A soft white braided garland could be a frame to announce Baby's birth.

MATERIALS

- assorted pink fabrics for appliqués and background
- solid pink fabric for backing
- batting

SIZE
finished piece: 26 ³/₄" x 30 ³/₄" (67 x 77 cm)

TECHNIQUE
appliqué

INSTRUCTIONS

- Cut the 26 ³/₄" x 30 ³/₄" (67 x 77 cm) background.
- Cut and piece 3" (7.5 cm) squares to form a 21" (8.5 cm) strip-pieced row.
- Stitch the row to the top of the background.
- Appliqué a row of clamshells onto the strip-pieced row.
- Appliqué a second row of clamshells over the first, staggering them.
- Continue adding rows of clamshells until the background has been covered.
- Trim the edges of the outer clamshells even with the background.
- Cut the batting 26 ³/₄" x 30 ³/₄" (67 x 77 cm) and backing 32" x 36" (80 x 90cm).
- Layer the backing, batting, and top; baste, then quilt.
- Finish the edges by folding the backing onto the background; blind-stitch.

SUNBONNET SUE

MATERIALS

(for pillow)
- ecru fabric for appliqués and background
- pink and brown gingham fabrics for appliqués and border
- fabric for pillow back
- interlining
- polyester fiberfill for stuffing

SIZE
finished pillow: 12" (30 cm) square

TECHNIQUE
appliqué

Bedside floor mat

Pillow

INSTRUCTIONS

- Cut the 9 1/4" (23 cm) square background.
- Cut out and appliqué Sun Bonnet Sue onto the background.
- Cut and join to the background the 1 3/8" (3.5 cm) border.
- Cut the batting and interlining 12" (30 cm) square.
- Layer the pillow top and batting; baste.
- Cut the 12" (30 cm) pillow back, then stitch it to the pillow top, right sides facing, leaving an opening in one edge for turning.
- Turn the pillow right side out, stuff it with fiberfill, then whip-stitch the opening closed.

Sunbonnet Sue appliqué blocks are framed alternately with pink and brown on this mini-quilt finished with a sawtooth border. (Coin)

COVERLET/BABY CARRIER

MATERIALS

- light blue gingham fabric for background and ties
- assorted pink and blue fabrics for appliqués
- batting
- backing

SIZE
finished coverlet: 34" x 21 $\frac{1}{4}$" (85 x 53 cm)

TECHNIQUE
appliqué

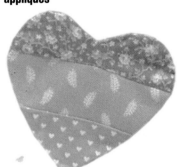

INSTRUCTIONS

- Cut the 34" x 21 $\frac{1}{4}$" (85 x 53 cm) background.
- Cut and make strip-pieced fabric, then cut out the hearts from it.
- Appliqué the hearts onto the background.
- Cut the batting 34" x 21 $\frac{1}{4}$" (85 x 53 cm) and backing 38" x 25 $\frac{1}{4}$" (95 x 63 cm).
- Layer the backing, batting, and top; baste, then quilt.
- Finish the edges by turning the backing over the background to form a 1" (2.5 cm) border.
- Cut and stitch two $\frac{7}{8}$" (2 cm) doubled ties, then sew them to the bottom corners of the coverlet.

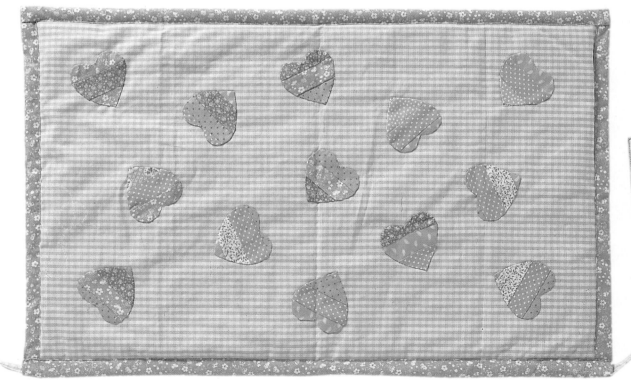

*The coverlet/carrier is
shown both flat and
folded. (G. Berti)*

HEARTS

MATERIALS

- ecru fabric for block backgrounds and backing
- assorted fabrics for appliqués, lattice, and borders
- batting

SIZE
block: 7 $\frac{1}{4}$" (18cm) square
finished piece: 42 $\frac{1}{4}$" x 51 $\frac{1}{2}$" (107 x 130 cm)

TECHNIQUES
American and appliqué

INSTRUCTIONS

- Cut the 7 $\frac{1}{4}$" (18 cm) blocks.
- Cut out and appliqué the hearts onto the blocks.
- Cut out 2" (5 cm) lattice strips and connecting squares.
- Join the blocks and vertical lattice to form rows.

- Join the rows and horizontal lattice to form the 35" x 44 $\frac{1}{4}$" (87 x 110 cm) quilt center.
- Cut and join to the quilt center the 2" (5 cm) inner border and the 1 $\frac{5}{8}$" (4 cm) outer border.
- Cut the batting 42 $\frac{1}{4}$" x 51 $\frac{1}{2}$" (107 x 130 cm) and backing 44 $\frac{1}{4}$" x 53 $\frac{1}{2}$" (110 x 134 cm).
- Layer the backing, batting, and top; baste, then quilt.
- Finish the edges by folding the backing over the outer border; blind-stitch.

G. Berti

S. Ognibene

BOYS AND GIRLS TOGETHER

MATERIALS

- ecru fabric for block backgrounds and outer border
- dark green fabric for inner border and backing
- assorted fabrics for appliqués
- batting

SIZE
finished piece: 41 $\frac{1}{4}$" x 47 $\frac{1}{4}$" (103 x 118 cm)

TECHNIQUES
American and appliqué

INSTRUCTIONS

- Cut 10" x 6" (25 x 15 cm) rectangles for the walls.
- Cut 10" x 2" (25 x 5 cm) rectangles for the windowsills.
- Cut and join assorted 2" (5 cm) squares to form a 10" (25 cm) square checkerboard.
- Join the walls, windowsills, and checkerboards to form 3 rows.
- Join the rows to form the 30" x 36" (75 x 90 cm) quilt center.
- Cut and appliqué the children on all but the bottom row.
- Cut and join to the quilt center the 1 $\frac{5}{8}$" (4 cm) inner border and 4" (10 cm) outer border.
- Cut the batting 41 $\frac{1}{4}$" x 47 $\frac{1}{4}$" (103 x 118 cm) and backing 44" x 50" (110 x 125 cm).
- Layer the backing, batting, and top; baste, then quilt.
- Finish the edges by folding the backing over the border; blind-stitch.

M. Jordan

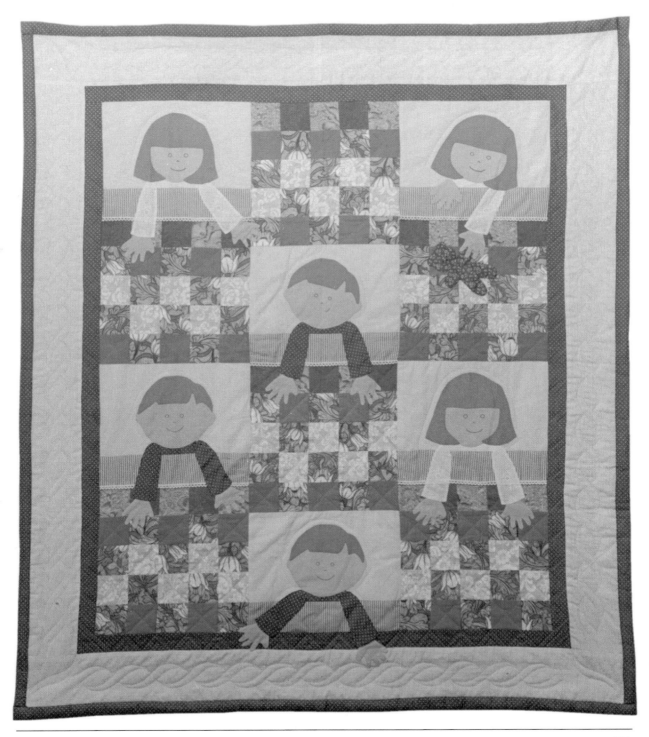

STENCILED STARS

MATERIALS

- **white and light blue solid fabrics for blocks**
- **white-and-light-blue print fabrics for lattice and border**
- **medium blue fabric for lattice squares and backing**
- **batting**
- **blue acrylic paint**

SIZE
block: 5 $^5/_8$" (14 cm) square
finished piece: 25 $^1/_4$" x 32 $^5/_8$" (64 x 82 cm)

TECHNIQUE:
American

INSTRUCTIONS

- *Cut 5 $^5/_8$" (14 cm) squares for the blocks.*
- *Use acrylic paint to stencil the stars on the blocks.*
- *Cut the 1 $^5/_8$" (4 cm) lattice strips and squares.*
- *Join the blocks, vertical lattice, and lattice squares to form rows.*
- *Join the rows, horizontal lattice, and lattice squares to form the 27 $^5/_8$" x 20 $^1/_4$" (69 x 51 cm) quilt center.*
- *Cut and join to the quilt center the 2 $^1/_2$" (6 cm) border.*
- *Cut the batting 25 $^1/_4$" x 32 $^5/_8$" (64 x 82 cm) and backing 28" x 36" (70 x 88 cm).*
- *Layer the backing, batting, and top; baste, then quilt.*
- *Finish the edges by folding the backing over the border; blind-stitch.*

CHECKERED BANNER

MATERIALS

- assorted white-on-blue fabrics for square patches
- blue-on-white fabric for triangular patches, border, and tabs
- batting
- backing

SIZE
finished banner: 53 ³/₄" x 22 ⁵/₈" (133 x 56 cm)

TECHNIQUE
American

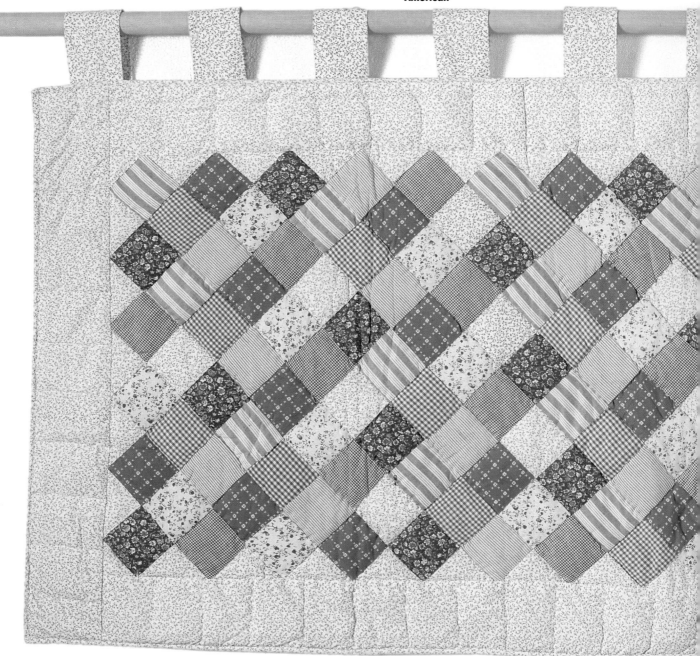

INSTRUCTIONS

- Use the Quick & Easy method to cut 2" (5 cm) and 1 3/8" (3.5 cm) squares and triangles.
- Join the squares and triangles to form rows.
- Join the rows to make the 47 5/8" x 16 7/8" (119 x 42 cm) quilt center.
- Cut and join to the quilt center the 2 7/8" (7 cm) border.
- Cut 4" (10 cm) strips, fold them in half lengthwise, and stitch.
- Fold the strips in half crosswise to form the tabs, then pin and baste them to the top border on the front of the quilt.
- Cut the 53 3/4" x 22 5/8" (133 x 56 cm) batting and backing.
- Layer the quilt top and batting; baste.
- Stitch the backing to the quilt top, over the tabs, right sides facing, leaving an opening in the bottom edge for turning.
- Turn the quilt right side out; whip-stitch the opening closed.

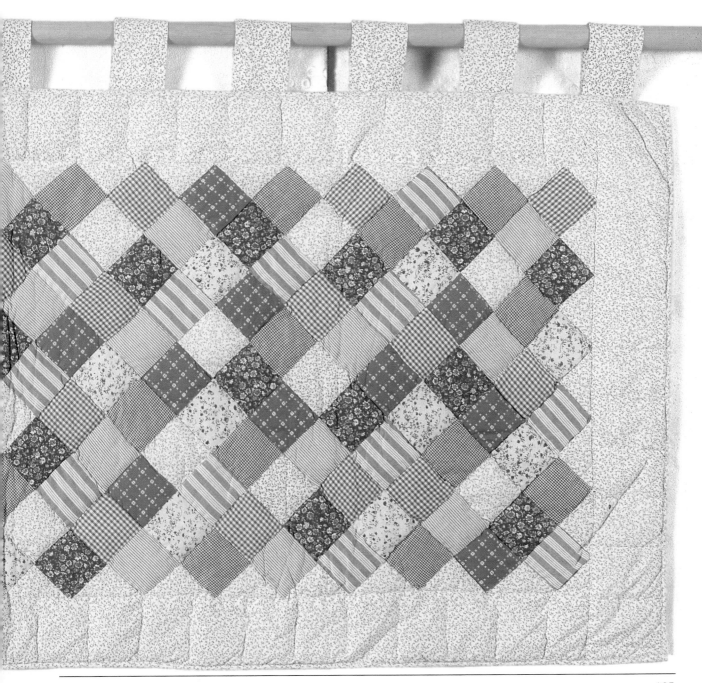

RAIL FENCE

MATERIALS

- pale, light, and medium green fabrics for blocks
- red-and-green fabrics for inner and outer borders
- dark green fabric for middle border
- batting
- backing

SIZE
block: 4 $^7/_8$" (12 cm) square
finished piece: 39 $^1/_4$" x 58 $^3/_8$" (98 x 146 cm)

TECHNIQUE
American
The Rail Fence motif resembles a zigzag and may be made in several different techniques. The coverlet, opposite, was made of strip-pieced fabric.

INSTRUCTIONS

- Cut and join 1 $^5/_8$" (4 cm) strips to make three 4 $^7/_8$" (12 cm) rows.
- From these rows cut 4 $^7/_8$" (12 cm) strip-pieced squares.
- Join the pieced squares, alternating horizontal and vertical patches, to form rows.
- Join the rows to make the 33 $^5/_8$" x 52 $^7/_8$" (84 x 132 cm) quilt center.
- Cut and join to the quilt center the $^7/_8$" (2 cm) inner border, the 4" (10 cm) middle border, and the $^7/_8$" (2 cm) outer border, including 2" (5 cm) for finishing.
- Cut the batting and backing 39 $^1/_4$" x 58 $^3/_8$" (98 x 146 cm).
- Layer the backing, batting, and top; baste, then quilt.
- Finish the edges by folding the outer border over the backing; blind-stitch.

Stacks of coordinating fabrics, particularly useful when making strip-pieced fabric.

G. Berti

PRAIRIE HOUSES

MATERIALS

- assorted pink, white, and blue fabrics for blocks, lattice, borders, and backing
- batting

SIZE
block: 5 5/8" x 4 7/8" (14 x 12 cm)
finished piece: 32 1/4" x 35" (80 x 100 cm)

TECHNIQUE
English or tracing paper

INSTRUCTIONS

- Cut and piece the 5 5/8" x 4 7/8" (14 x 12 cm) house blocks.
- Cut the 2" (5 cm) horizontal lattice and 2 3/8" (6 cm) vertical lattice.

- Join the blocks and vertical lattice to form rows.
- Join the rows and horizontal lattice to form the 21 3/4" x 24 1/2" (54 x 61 cm) quilt center.
- Cut and join the 2 3/8" (6 cm) first border to the quilt top.
- Cut and join to the quilt center the 7/8" (2 cm) second, third, and fourth borders.
- Cut the batting 32 1/4" x 35" (80 x 100 cm) and backing 35" x 38" (90 x 110 cm).
- Layer the backing, batting, and top; baste, then quilt.
- Finish the edges by folding the backing over the outermost border; blind-stitch.

These pajama holders were made in colors to match the coverlet. Both Sue and Sam versions have a zipper on the back and hanging ties. (E. Santini)

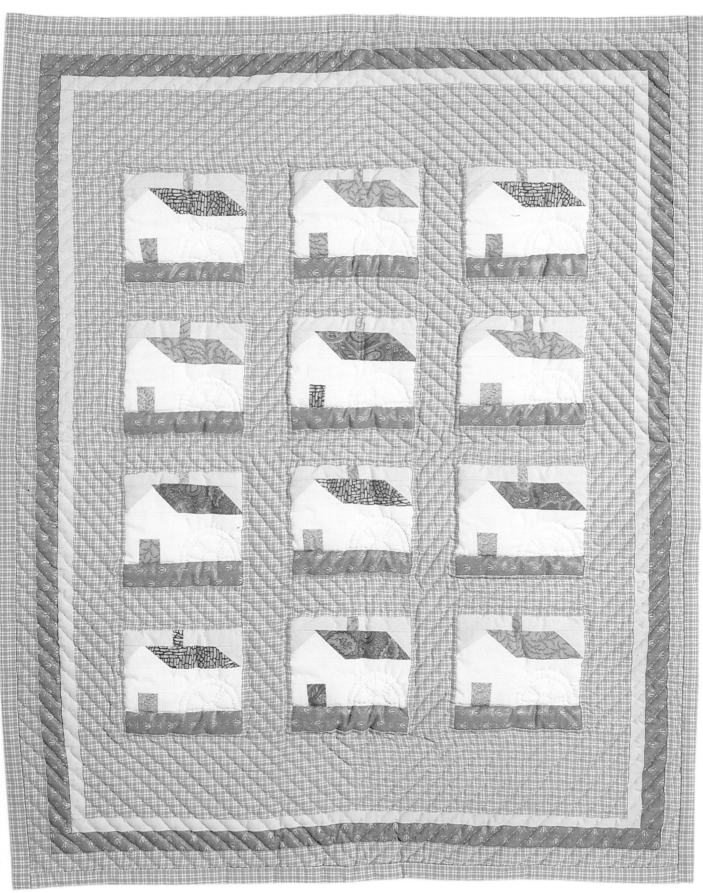

G. Berti

SEMINOLE STRIPS

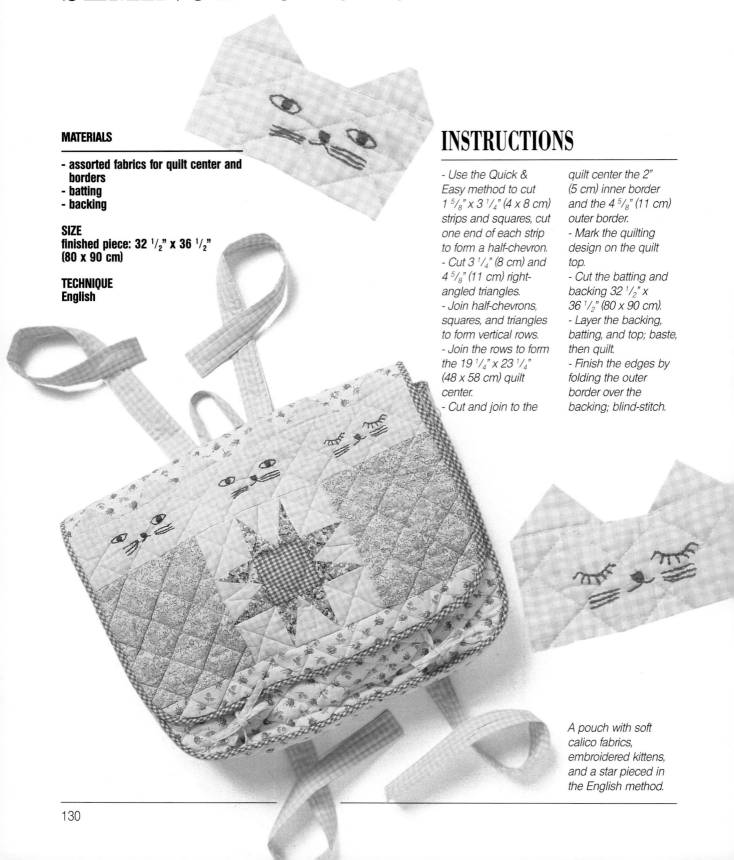

MATERIALS

- assorted fabrics for quilt center and borders
- batting
- backing

SIZE
finished piece: 32 $\frac{1}{2}$" x 36 $\frac{1}{2}$"
(80 x 90 cm)

TECHNIQUE
English

INSTRUCTIONS

- Use the Quick & Easy method to cut 1 $\frac{5}{8}$" x 3 $\frac{1}{4}$" (4 x 8 cm) strips and squares, cut one end of each strip to form a half-chevron.
- Cut 3 $\frac{1}{4}$" (8 cm) and 4 $\frac{5}{8}$" (11 cm) right-angled triangles.
- Join half-chevrons, squares, and triangles to form vertical rows.
- Join the rows to form the 19 $\frac{1}{4}$" x 23 $\frac{1}{4}$" (48 x 58 cm) quilt center.
- Cut and join to the quilt center the 2" (5 cm) inner border and the 4 $\frac{5}{8}$" (11 cm) outer border.
- Mark the quilting design on the quilt top.
- Cut the batting and backing 32 $\frac{1}{2}$" x 36 $\frac{1}{2}$" (80 x 90 cm).
- Layer the backing, batting, and top; baste, then quilt.
- Finish the edges by folding the outer border over the backing; blind-stitch.

A pouch with soft calico fabrics, embroidered kittens, and a star pieced in the English method.

V. Grassi

CRAZY QUILT

MATERIALS

- ground fabric
- assorted fabrics for patches and block backgrounds
- assorted tiny ginghams for ruffle
- batting
- backing
- narrow red ribbon

SIZE
block: 9" (23 cm) square
finished piece: 27" x 36" (67 x 90 cm) plus trim

TECHNIQUE
Crazy quilting

INSTRUCTIONS

- Cut 9" (23 cm) squares for the block backgrounds.
- Cover each background with random patches.
- Join the blocks to form rows.
- Join the rows to form the 27" x 36" (67 x 90 cm) quilt top.
- Use embroidery thread to decoratively stitch over the seams.

- Cut and join 3 $\frac{1}{4}$" (8 cm) ruffle strips; press the ruffle in half lengthwise, right side out.
- Attach the doubled ruffle to the outer edge of the quilt top.
- Cut the batting and backing 27" x 36" (67 x 90 cm).
- Layer the backing, batting, and top; baste, then quilt.
- Finish off the edges by folding the backing to the inside, covering the ruffle seam; blind-stitch.
- Tie tiny bows, then sew them to the front of the quilt at the intersections of the blocks.

A small Crazy Quilt pillow.

KITTENS

MATERIALS

- assorted fabrics for blocks
- ecru fabric for background and outer border
- batting
- backing

SIZE
block: 3 $\frac{1}{4}$" (8 cm) square
finished quilt: 56" x 100 $\frac{7}{8}$" (140 x 252 cm)

TECHNIQUE
tracing paper

INSTRUCTIONS

- Cut and piece the 3 $\frac{1}{4}$" (8 cm) square and 3 $\frac{1}{4}$" x 9 $\frac{3}{4}$" (8 x 24 cm) rectangular kitten blocks.
- Join the blocks to form rows.
- Join the rows to form the 48" x 92 $\frac{7}{8}$" (120 x 232 cm) quilt center.
- Cut and join to the quilt center the $\frac{1}{4}$" (0.5 cm) inner border and the 2" (5 cm) outer border.
- Cut the batting 56" x 100 $\frac{7}{8}$" (140 x 252 cm) and backing 60 $\frac{7}{8}$" x 105 $\frac{5}{8}$" (152 x 264 cm).
- Layer the backing, batting, and top; baste, then quilt.

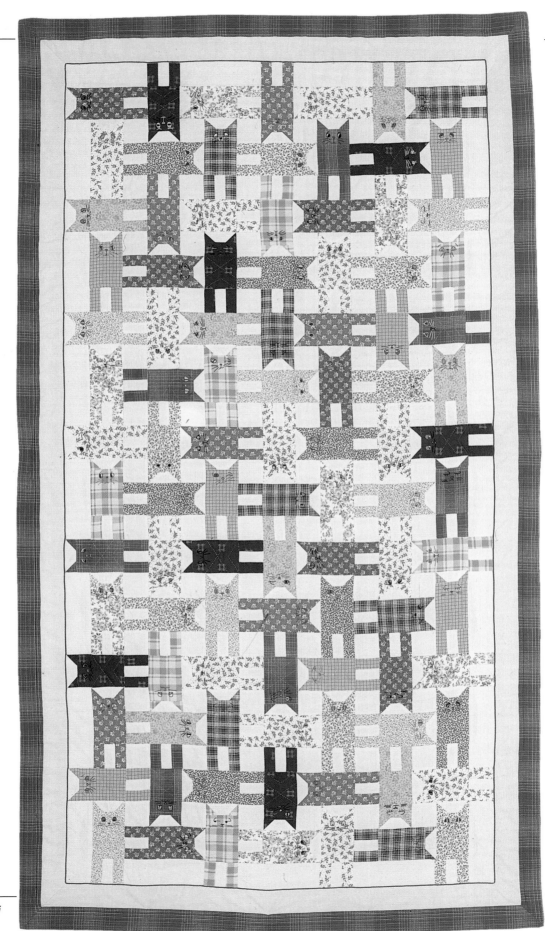

ROCKING HORSE TOTE BAG

A bag and accessories in matching fabrics. (E. Santini)

MATERIALS

- burgundy and ecru striped and checked fabrics
- burgundy solid for appliqué
- cording
- embroidery floss, burgundy

SIZE
**finished bag: 12" x 14"
(30 x 35 cm)**

TECHNIQUE
appliqué

INSTRUCTIONS

- Cut the 24" x 14" (60 x 35 cm) bag.
- Cut and appliqué the rocking horse.
- Make the embroidery-floss horse tail.
- Fold the bag in half crosswise, then seam both side edges.
- Make a casing at the upper edge of the bag, insert the cording, and knot the ends together.

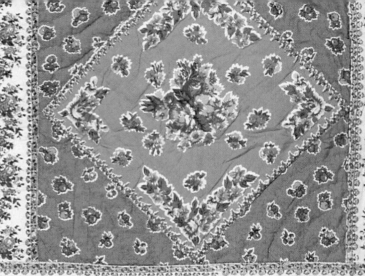
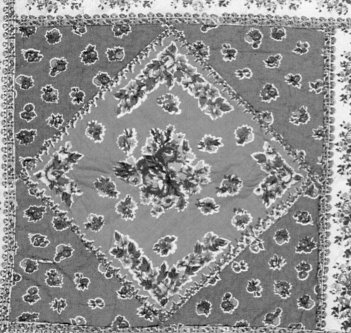

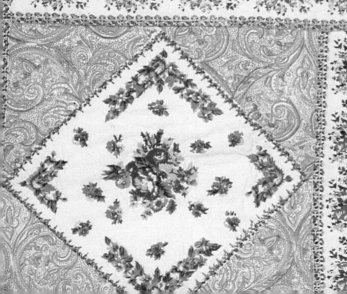
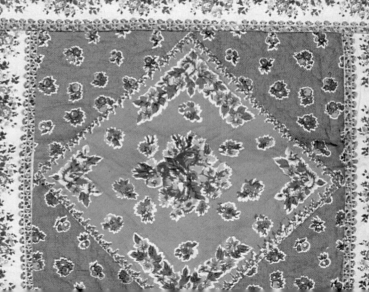

BIG IDEAS
FOR SMALL
PRESENTS

PIGLET PAINTER

Mini-quilt with appliquéd landscape. (Coin)

COUNTRY HOUSES

On this soft-toned coverlet the house blocks are pieced in mirror images with assorted fabrics.
(Coin)

CIRCUS TIME

*Pieced and appliquéd animals and clowns
will be the stars of Baby's dreams.
(G. Musiari from* Tender Loving Covers*).*

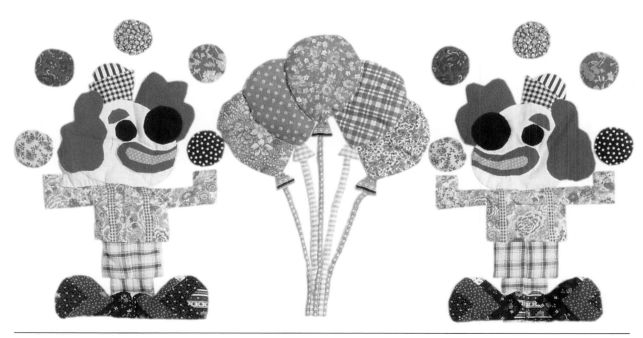

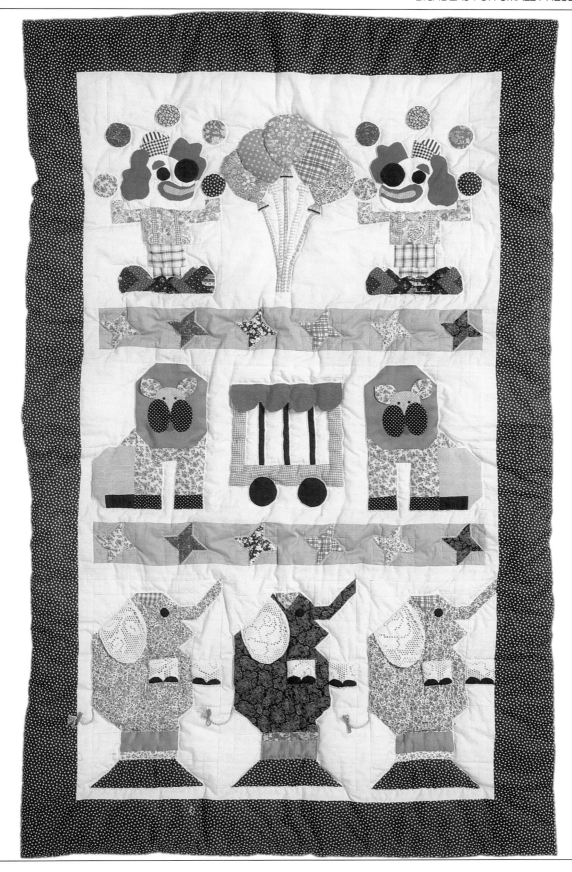

AUTUMN SCARECROW

This mini-quilt made in warm colors has a different appliquéd symbol of autumn on each block. Plain lattice strips join the blocks to form the quilt center.

APPLE CIDER

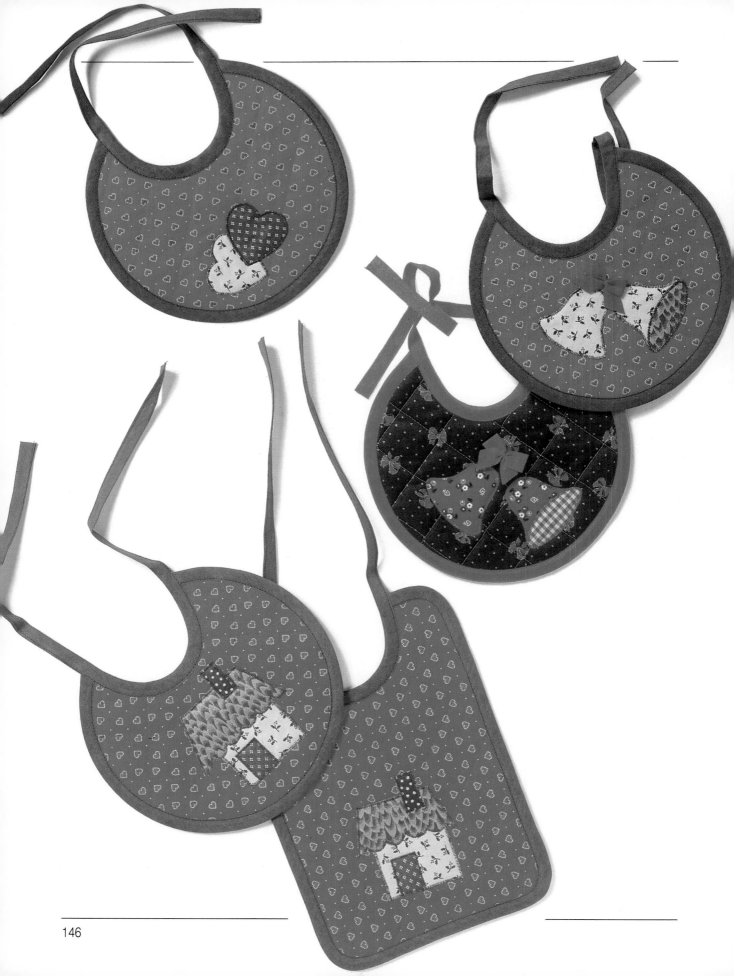

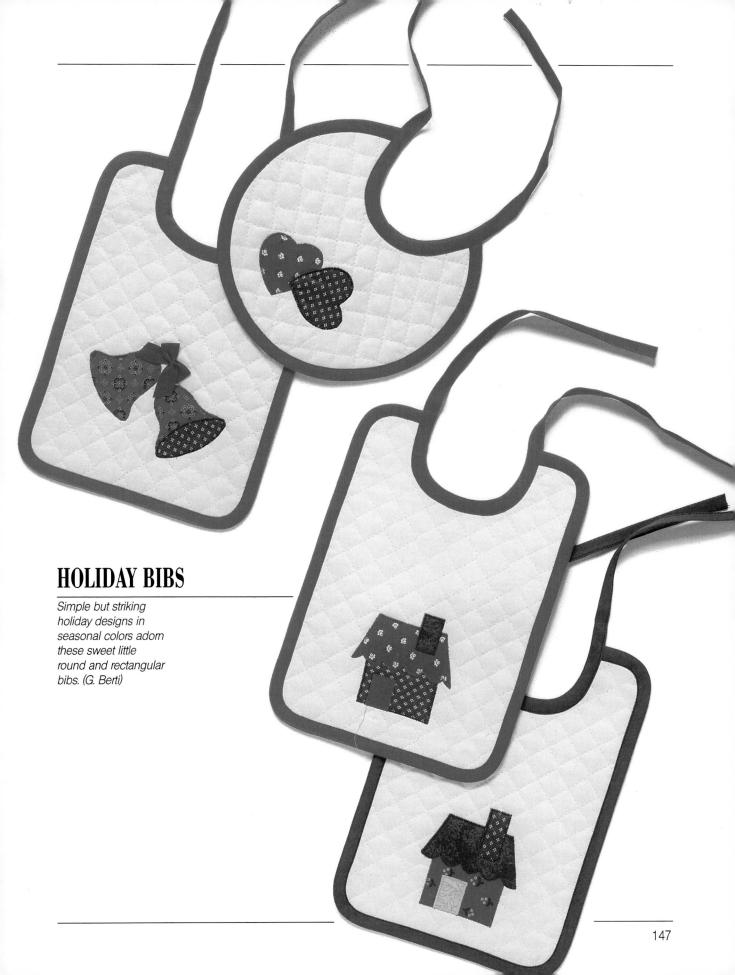

HOLIDAY BIBS

*Simple but striking
holiday designs in
seasonal colors adorn
these sweet little
round and rectangular
bibs. (G. Berti)*

LOG CABIN FRAME

In the center of each Log Cabin is a single motif. A pink-and-green Log Cabin frames a reproduction of Baby on fabric. (G. Berti)

ESPECIALLY FOR HER

Pretty-in-pink Log Cabin motifs decorate this photo album and pocketed pinafore. (G. Berti)

A hand-appliquéd train chugs across this pink gingham sundress. (P. Visioli)

Slippers and slipper-bag with appliquéd soft pink hearts. (E. Santini)

ESPECIALLY FOR HIM

This mini-quilt has blocks of varying shapes and sizes, each decorated with simple but colorful appliqués that Baby will love. (Coin)

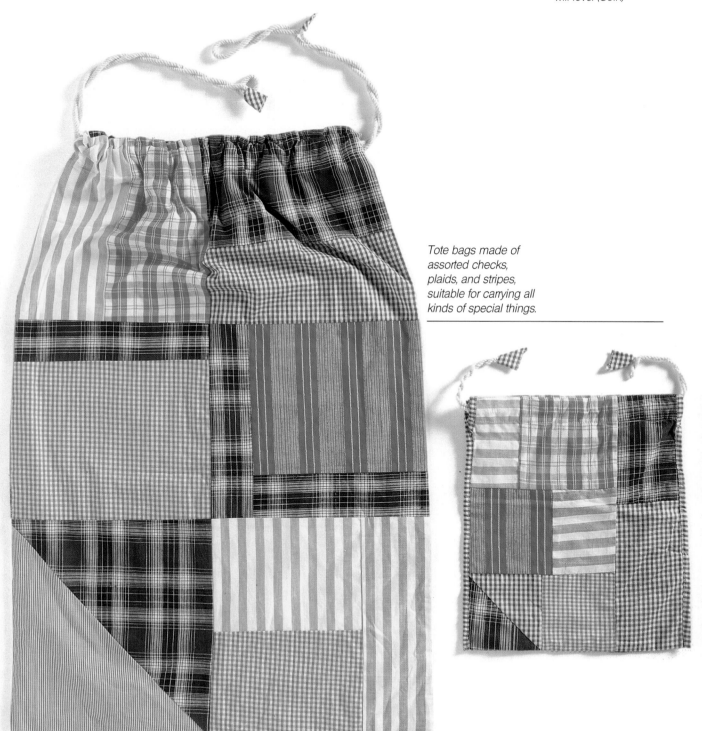

Tote bags made of assorted checks, plaids, and stripes, suitable for carrying all kinds of special things.

BABY'S FIRST TABLE SETTING

*Stuffed kittens keep
Baby company at a
place setting
embellished with kitten
and teddy-bear
appliqués.
(E. Santini)*

PROJECT
PATTERNS

The project patterns on the following pages can be enlarged on a photocopier to any desired size.

DUCKLINGS

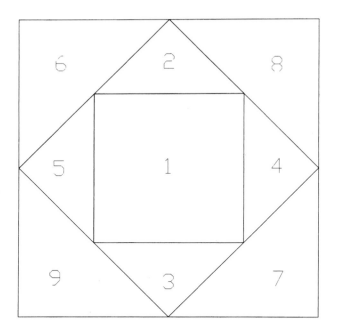

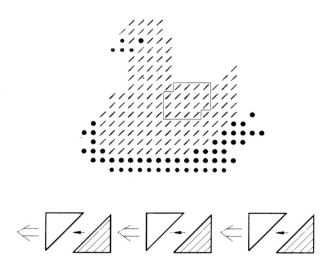

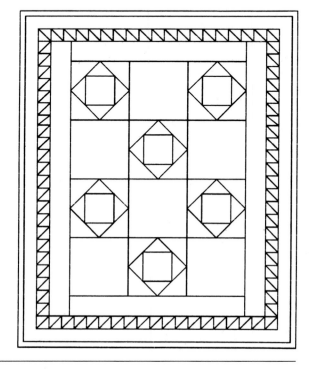

DRESSES

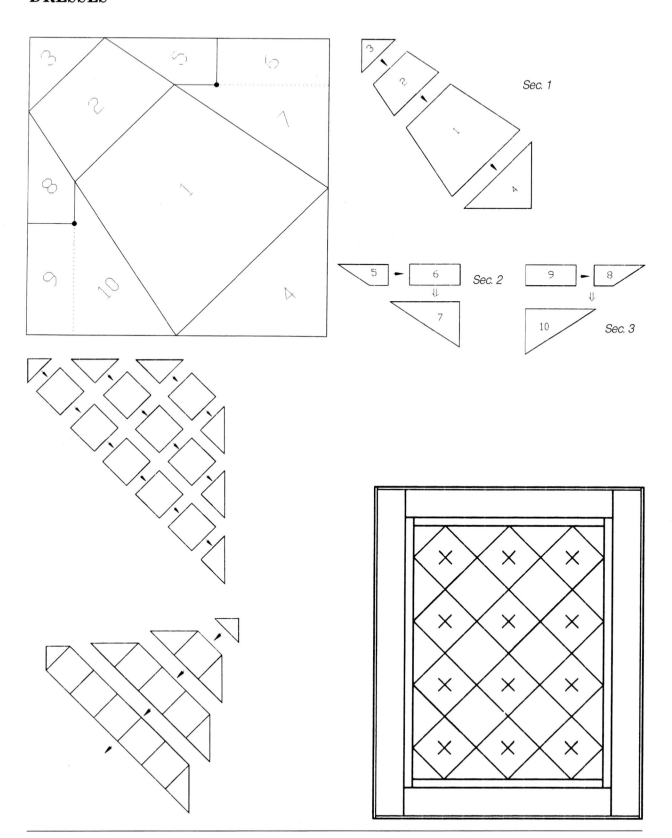

Sec. 1

Sec. 2

Sec. 3

CABIN IN THE WOODS

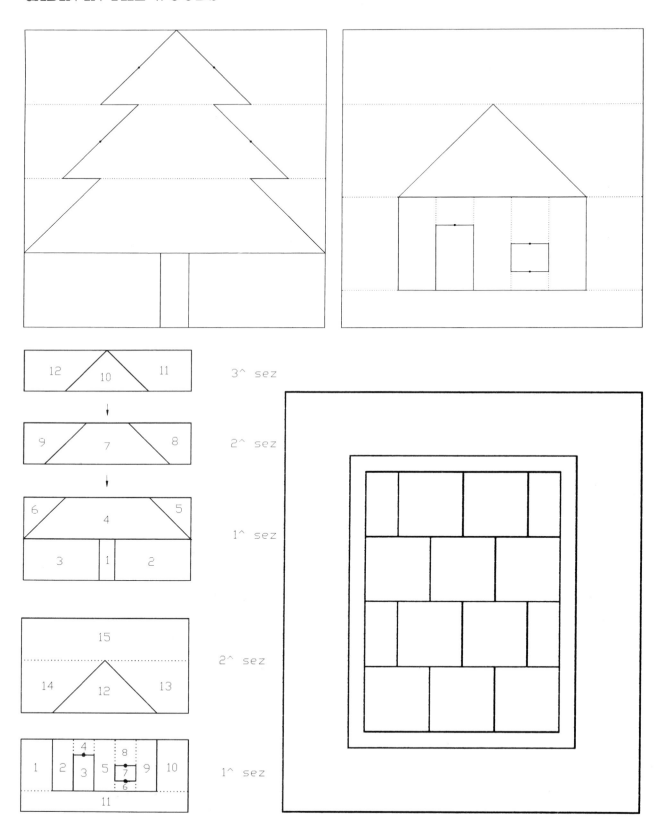

3^ sez

2^ sez

1^ sez

2^ sez

1^ sez

VILLAGE

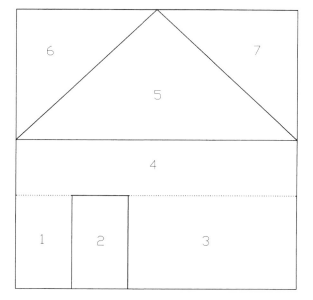

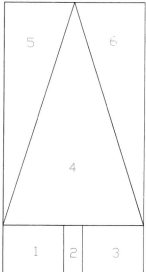

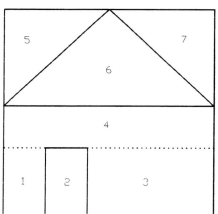

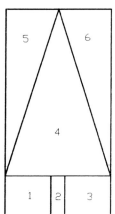

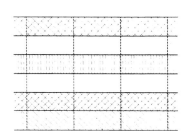

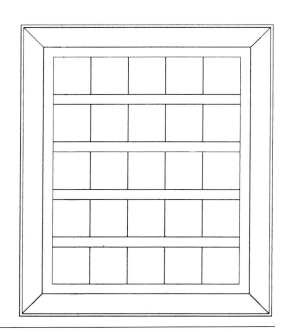

"BUONA NOTTE"

PINK HOUSES

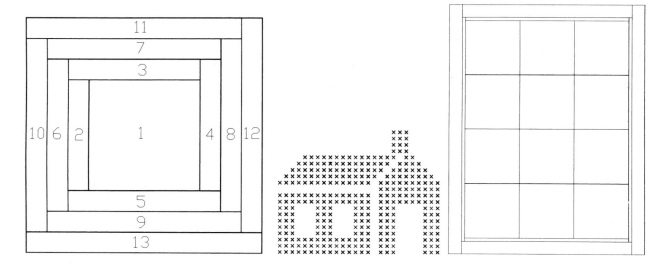

PINWHEELS

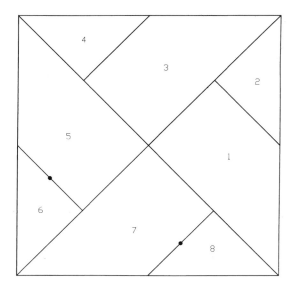

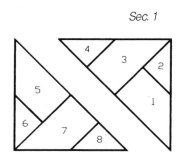

Sec. 1

Sec. 2

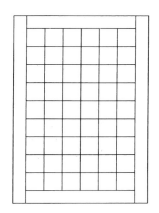

VIOLETS IN LOG CABINS

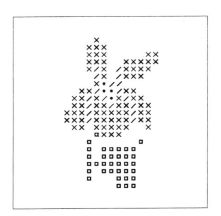

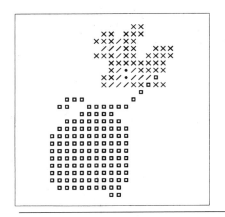

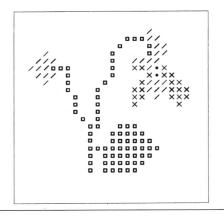

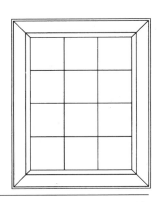

SUE 'N' SAM

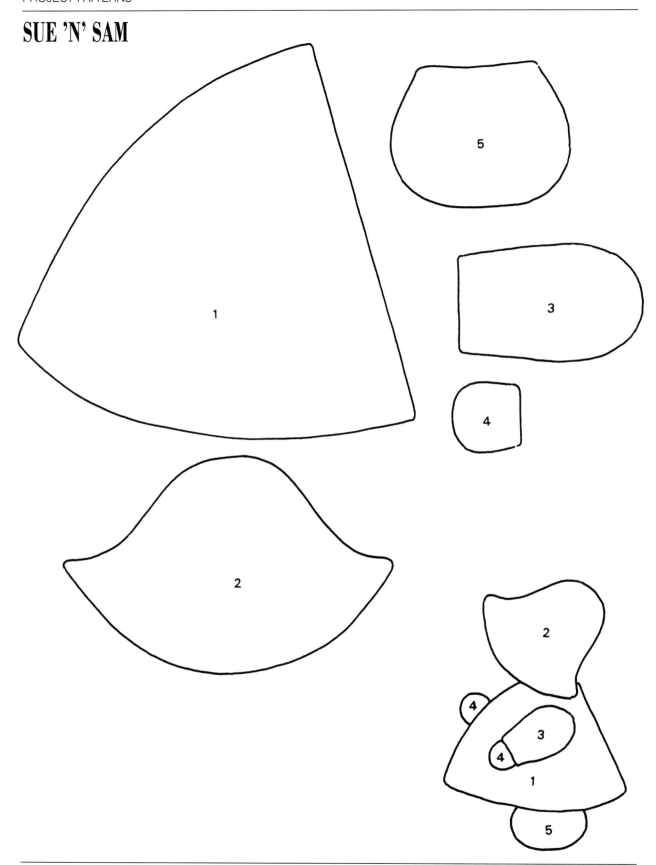

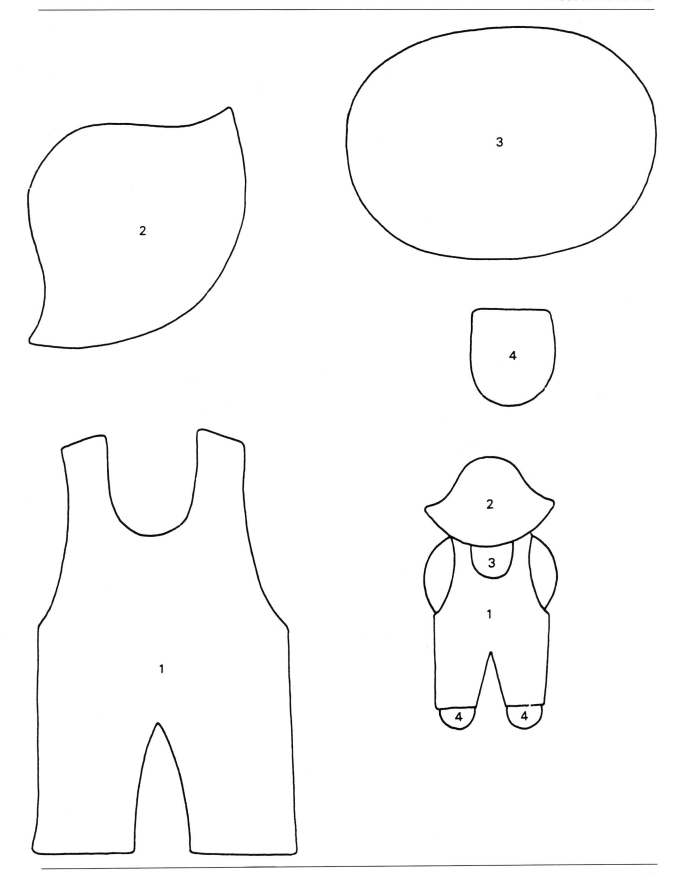

BUNNIES

CUPS AND SAUCERS

TEDDY BEARS

BABY BUGGIES

LACE-TRIMMED BASSINET

TREE SKIRT

CLAMSHELLS

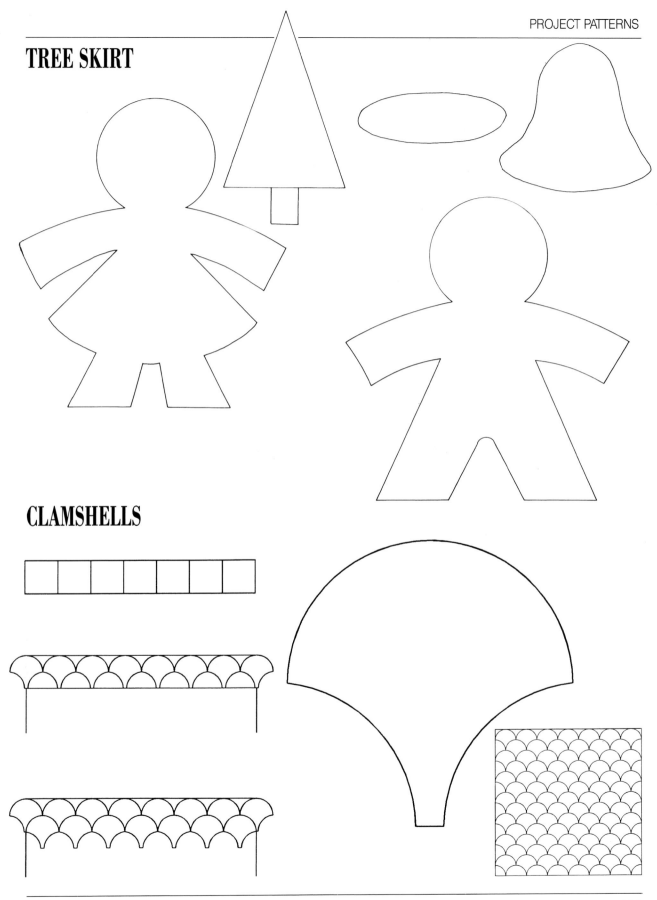

SUNBONNET SUE

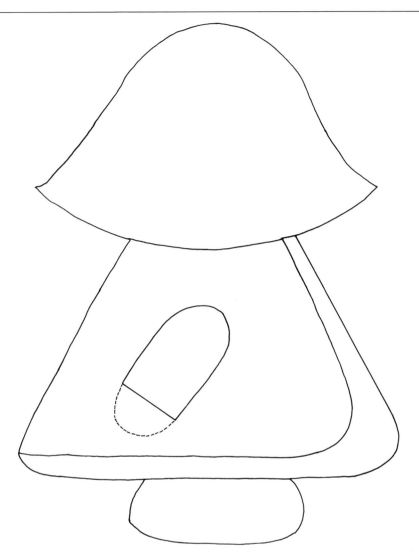

HEARTS

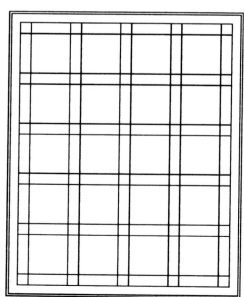

COVERLET/
BABY CARRIER

BOYS AND GIRLS TOGETHER

CHECKERED BANNER

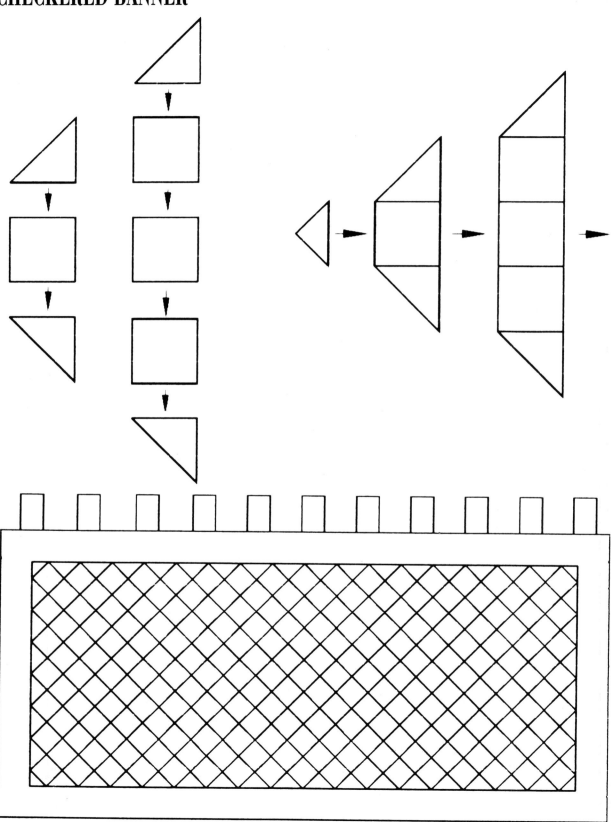

RAIL FENCE

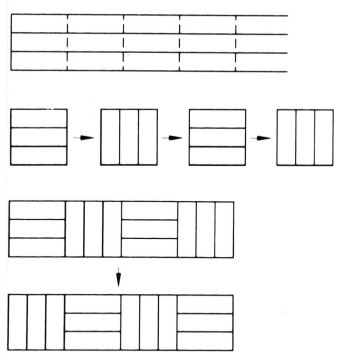

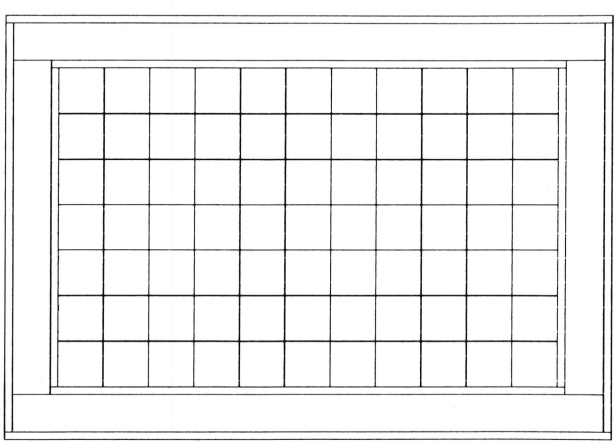

PRAIRIE HOUSES

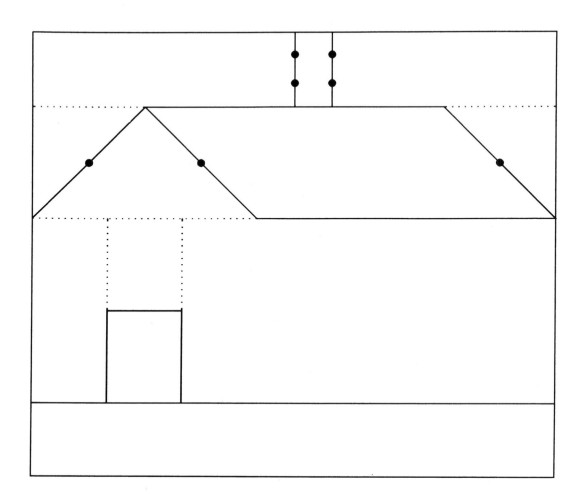

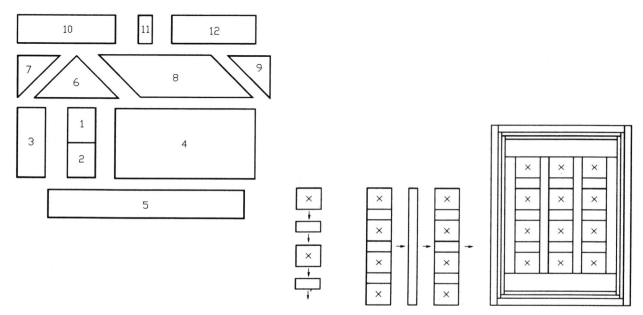

SEMINOLE STRIPS

KITTENS

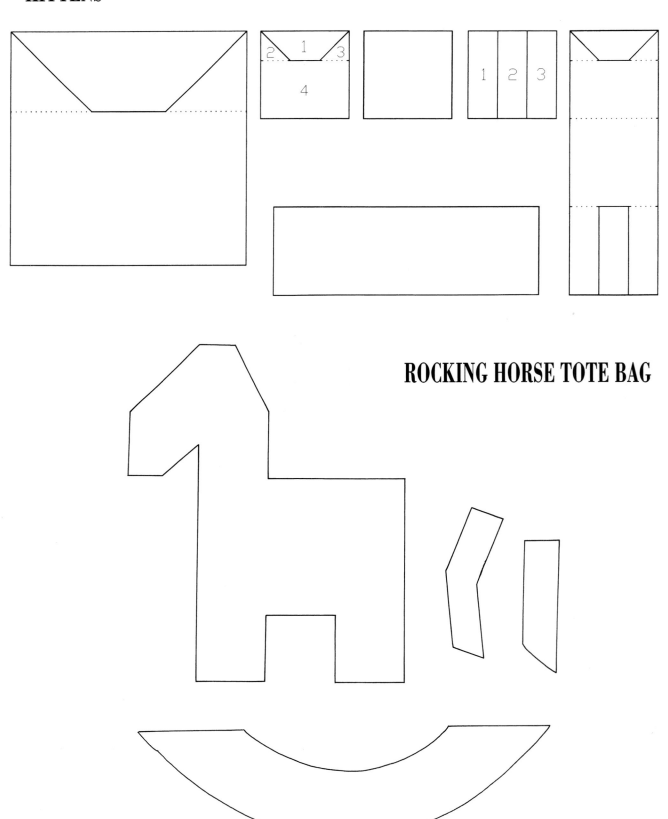

ROCKING HORSE TOTE BAG

INDEX